Foreword Clarion 4 Star Review

Carr's voice is compassionate and pastoral, and as a former educator and experienced preacher, he conveys ideas in a clear and logical manner, with each idea building firmly on the last, leading step by step to deeper faith. Carr's voice is relentlessly positive and faith-filled, but it's not naïve or oblivious in any way. What he shares is rooted in his own pain and learning, and that earnestness comes through on the page, to the benefit of readers. *As Sparks Fly Upward prompts Christians to learn to see life beyond the surface, beyond the events that take place, and instead view life through faith in God.*

BlueInk Red Starr Review

Michael Carr's *As Sparks Fly Upward* is an impressive, thoughtful, and poetic collection of writings, reflections, and sermons that should serve as a source of inspiration for readers who are experiencing strife and turmoil. Carr has the soul of an artist. Like any great artist, his honesty can be raw. "Being a Christian is not the life of a sissy. All who profess [Jesus'] name will live through hazardous experiences that are the guarantee of discipleship." These can be tough words to hear, yet, Carr, who has endured much in his 80-plus years, *speaks as one who knows that truth ultimately leads to liberation.*

AS SPARKS FLY UPWARD

Weathering the Storms of Life

Michael Carr

authorHOUSE®

AuthorHouse™ UK
1663 Liberty Drive
Bloomington, IN 47403 USA
www.authorhouse.co.uk
Phone: 0800.197.4150

Published by AuthorHouse 11/10/2016

ISBN: 978-1-5246-3056-0 (sc)
ISBN: 978-1-5246-3054-6 (hc)
ISBN: 978-1-5246-3055-3 (e)

Print information available on the last page.

Contents

Foreword

I have had the privilege of knowing Michael Carr for over two decades, often ministering alongside him, and have counted him for years as a dear friend. Our first meeting, however, was a poor indication of the friendship that was to develop. He had invited me to do a weekend seminar at his church in Harrow, London – Harrow International Christian Centre. The problem was he had invited me sight unseen based on the encouragement of a mutual friend.

I walked in to his church for the first meeting with long hair and wearing Doc Martens boots and black jeans and smacking of the Southern California alternative culture. Michael came across to me as the polar opposite. He was, to my mind, the quintessential conservative British aristocratic type, from his suit and voice to the way he wore his reading glasses perched on the end of his nose. I never would have guessed that Michael and his wife at the time, Patricia, would become such great friends to me.

I quickly came to deeply appreciate that Michael was a 'man of the Word' with a deep love for the presence of God and seeing the gifts of the Holy Spirit in action. By 'man of the Word' I do not merely mean a theologian or one who had memorised a lot of Bible verses. He is that, but he is much more. He is a leader in the body of Christ, who is growing increasingly rarer. Michael lives, thinks, acts, and speaks according to the principals, ways, and truths of God as given to us in the Bible. In an age where far too many leaders are 'led' by current trends of church growth and cultural values, Michael, for decades, has been a true Christ-focused pastor and teacher who cared far more about representing the kingdom of God than the cultural realms of the hour.

As Sparks Fly Upwards is an outstanding biblical work in and of itself. It is more than that, though. It is a testimony of how one man given over to a lifetime of seeking first the kingdom of God has lived his life, often in the midst of amazing challenges. As Michael refers quite often to his first wife, Pat, throughout the book, he paints a living picture of what it means to let God shape and mould oneself while facing ongoing difficulties. While Patricia was an amazing woman of God, she also fought lifelong health issues that too often were life threatening. While many men would have given up on their ministry, their wife, or even their faith Michael gives us a living example of how to live out Philippians 2:1–8. Michael has lived a life of sacrifice, preferring, and caring for others throughout long difficult seasons.

In all the times I have been ministering as a guest speaker at HICC (Harrow International Christian Centre) I never had the privilege of hearing Michael give a full sermon. During many, many meetings over the years, however, I have witnessed Michael encouraging the church to take in what I was speaking on and focused on while ministering. And in those five-minute 'mini-sermons' Michael gave before or after I ministered, I was always aware of two things – one, Michael was able to pack more takeaway truths in those five minutes that I could give in thirty, and two, the church truly loves Michael.

They do not love him merely because of his charisma or style of teaching. They love him because, when he stands before them, they experience the unique Christlike blend of compassion, wisdom, and authority that God has brought about in Michael's life through years of being a man of the Word in the fullest sense.

We live in an age I often refer to as the 'quick fix, microwave and Internet age'. By that, I mean too many give up on things like jobs, relationships, families, and the like because they are not willing to pay the price to see things through to a successful conclusion. *As Sparks Fly Upwards* is a strong biblical encouragement to learn to see the trials and difficulties of life through the lens of God's wisdom and promises. As Michael tackles themes such as consolation in confusion and God redeeming our catastrophes, he does so with both wit and humility.

We can relate to Michael's stories not because we have experienced the same but, rather, because Michael constantly writes with both truth and humility. Michael is never guilty of pontificating or speaking down to his reader. As he relates his own journeys and learning to listen to the Holy Spirit and trust God's promises, we find we can relate our own battles to Michael's and have faith for the breakthroughs he has experienced.

As well, an additional aspect of Michael comes through in a very clear way throughout this book. And that is the truth that Jesus came that we might have life abundantly (John 10:10). Even in the midst of the thievery the devil often manages, there is still the righteousness, peace, and joy of the Holy Spirit God always intends for us to live out of. Michael's stories, points, and conclusion always point to the quality of life we can have in Christ, even in the face of adversity. It is a true joy to me to know that Michael and his second wife, Pamela, are still going strong, enjoying ministry, life, and romance, even in his eighties!

As I mentioned, Michael is a man of principal. *As Sparks Fly Upwards* strongly and thoroughly unpacks many of the essential ways of God that the short, warm and fuzzy, inspirational books of our day fail to do. *As Sparks Fly Upwards* will prove to many to demand a place on our bookshelves, always within reach. It will be for many a strong encouragement and tool, demonstrating how to live a life conformed to the image of Christ.

Marc A. Dupont
Marc Dupont Ministries, Inc.

Introduction

Job speaks the obvious: 'Yet man is born to trouble as surely as sparks fly upward.'[1] Thus starts the book. The title is predominant; the daily vagaries that throng us are like walking through a forest's dappled shade of mingled light and dark. We wish it were not so, but it seems unavoidable. The unremitting trial of the day, the temptations, the torments, the terrors, and the tests we face during our walk on earth create an uncertainty and unreconciled doubt of God's intentions in our present life and for our anticipated future. We say, as did a father from the New Testament, 'I believe, help thou my unbelief.'[2]

Having been a preacher for sixty-one years, starting at age twenty, I believe I have sufficient wisdom now to describe the pathway of life, the way God directs and keeps us, and the principles of His love in action. I have written several chapters about God's unfolding attitude towards our situations, accentuating the messages with scripture. And I offer no apology for doing that, for God's Word reigns in all circumstances of life for those who profess a living faith. I have endeavoured not to preach to you, for I am told people no longer read sermons. But life is a sermon. And in my case, it is six foot three and covered in skin. It is what we do and how we live, as much as pontificating from a pulpit that matters. But it is, at this point in my life, almost impossible for me not to hold myself in a preaching stance, for such stance is woven into the psyche of the public teacher.

I was born into a working-class family, where money was tight. We were poor, but we didn't know it. We got on and lived and made ends meet. My father set us an example of hard work. There is no other way to live, for you only get out what you put in. I was the second son of three and named Michael, which means 'who is like God'. Who could possibly live up to that standard?! But being the second son was significant.

There is a scriptural law about the eldest son, who receives the double portion of his father's goods.[3] If the father had three sons, he divided his inheritance four ways, and the firstborn received two portions. This setup is neat for the firstborn but a bit iffy for the other two. However, there is also the law of the second son, for there is a trend in the Old Testament, which is significant and not often perceived. God's favour was not on Cain but on Abel, not Esau but Jacob, not Ishmael but Isaac, not Ephraim but Manasseh, not Aaron but Moses, not the first Adam but the last – Jesus Christ. I am a second son and have received of God's favour profusely. It is neither earned nor merited but is all of God. We have no cause to boast. God's favour is of grace. But frequently a thorn in the flesh is added to the blessing! Thus, 'God tutors through processes that are as varied as the men He calls.'[4]

I met my first wife when I was fifteen years old and she was thirteen at a Bible Class; we fell in love, got engaged, and I married her ten years later. We knew each other for sixty-five years and were married for fifty-four years. We had three children – two boys and a girl. But when she turned thirty-one, she developed myasthenia gravis, a very rare muscular disease. And the next twenty years were wiped out of our lives – we were to endure suffering, pain, physical weakness, anguish, and panic. She had a tracheotomy tube (trachi), a silver tube in her throat so she could breathe, and a gastrostomy tube in her stomach to eat, and she was wheelchair bound for several years. Some thorn!

In the midst of that trial, we built our first church, an independent Pentecostal assembly, which eventually joined Elim. I believed, like Paul the Apostle, that I should earn my living in the secular world. He was a tentmaker. I was a civil engineer. This held me in great stead to practically build a church, which I did – twice.

Because my wife was so ill, I gave up the church we had pioneered and also my lucrative job in the building industry and became a lecturer at Birmingham Polytechnic in building studies. I progressed to become the subject tutor in that discipline for three diplomas, which became first degrees when we became the University of Central England. I retired at age fifty and was called immediately to Kensington Temple, Notting Hill – Elim's top church in the metropolis. Nine months later, I was superintendent (bishop) of the Metropolitan Region for my movement, looking after fifty-five churches. And during that time, I built another pioneer work called the Harrow International Christian Centre (HICC) in the area where I resided.

I semi-retired from that assembly, becoming pastor emeritus in August 2015 at age eighty-one. The prognosis doctors had given my wife was that she would not reach middle age. But she died at seventy-eight in January 2014 from myasthenia and a brain tumour – a miracle of longevity, no doubt from God's goodness. I reasoned that a large, successful, multinational church like HICC needed a married couple to oversee it – women see more than men – so handed it over to my friend and his wife from Bristol. He had also had pioneered a dynamic church with limited facilities from its onset.

My initial experiences in the secular world – gaining credentials, working in the rough physical environments of building industry sites, and spending four years in a design office applying principles and developing for old and new builds, not to mention my life as a father to three rapidly growing children, along with keeping house and managing my sick wife – were, to say the least, severely fraught with unremitting demands. Later, during that period whilst a lecturer, I took a higher degree and a professional qualification at the chartered (royal) institute of building. In addition, I developed my own architectural practise. However, amid all the labour and involvement in the many aspects of my life, I made God my goal and demanded of myself that I would set apart two hours fellowship each day in *His presence*. It worked; I never had burn out or experienced physical exhaustion, except at bedtime, in spite of it all. He was my sure foundation, my tall strong tower, and my heart – beloved in all circumstances.

Through those decades of hard work, growing a family, nursing my wife, building churches and seeing people transformed, indelible principles were imparted and wrought in my life. These I will share with you. Watchman Nee, the Chinese writer, would call this book the 'Normal Christian Life'. I would call it 'Lifestyle Christianity'. Through everyday life, we traipse along God's pathway, meeting obstacles, adversities, perplexities, problems, and temptations and laughing because of joyous victories. Good or bad, black or white, high or low, days all figure in the writing of this book. The chapters differ as the years have passed, as with their passing, my maturity has grown and my understanding of God has become clearer – although in my humanity, I am still only able to hear God's whispers and edges of His acts and doings. We think we know, but then we realise we do not. We design our deft definitions, and that in itself limits God to the breadth of our limited understanding. And that which helps us also hinders us. All I can say is that we must dare to be remarkable, for in that stance and lifestyle, we many encounter God.

I refer to the scriptures constantly, for they are inspired and authoritative. Thus, the foundational aspects of all these book chapters are biblical, for the scitptures manifest divine wisdom – wisdom that created the earth and man and has set and holds all things in existence in motion. He, Jesus, is the living word, the expression of God, and the expectation of humanity. He lived before He was born and after He had died. He was an infant yet is the infinite Christ.

Chapter 1

Physostigma Venenosum

In 1840, missionaries reported the details of a macabre ritual practiced in the south-eastern corner of Nigeria:

> Those who were suspected of witchcraft, murder, and other terrible crimes were forced to swallow a bean that contained a deadly poison. If they died, which was more than likely, they were pronounced guilty. If they vomited up the bean and survived, they were innocent. Waverers who showed ill effects without expiring were sold into slavery.[5]

The missionaries regarded the *éséré* bean as a great social evil, simply because it was the chief means of so-called justice. The king had most plants that produced the bean destroyed but kept a few so he could monopolise the administration of justice. This scarcity was the major delay in identifying it.

During this period, adventurers, explorers, and missionaries scoured the globe for plants that would furnish new drugs, poisons, and useful chemicals. They brought coffee beans from Africa, the bark of cinchona trees from Peru, and the seeds of the East Indian tree *Strychnos nux-vomica*, from which chemists isolated caffeine, quinine, and strychnine. But for twenty years, the ingredients of *ésére*, the 'ordeal bean', eluded them because they couldn't identify the plant. However, in 1855, Reverend Waddell smuggled some seeds of the plant to Robert Christison in Edinburgh. They germinated but failed to produce flowers. Eventually, another missionary sent, preserved in alcohol, a plant that had grown successfully. The plant was named *Physostigma venenosum*.

Christison experimented with it. By swallowing some, he found it slowed his heart down and probably killed by paralysing the heart. British doctors began to realise that, in small quantities, the plant could have beneficial effects, for one of the ingredients was the alkaloid physostigmine. This could be used to counteract the lethal poison found in deadly nightshade, whose berries had been mistakenly eaten by children. Its swift application saved many lives.

Its additional benefit was to protect against germ warfare. In 1934, an assistant medical officer at St Alfege's Hospital in London, while searching for a cure for myasthenia gravis, a muscle-wasting disease, realised that the symptoms were much like curare poisoning, in which physostigmine was used as a cure. Myasthenia is an autoimmune disease in which the body produces antibodies against receptors for the neurotransmitters that make muscles contract, causing paralysis.

The effects of the nerve agent sarin, which was released by terrorists in March 1995 in a Tokyo subway, killing twelve people, are similar to those of myasthenia. Given the right dosage, the effects of the poison can be cured without lasting damage. British and American troops going into action are given pyridostigmine, a derivative of physostigmine that is now used for myasthenia. The Swiss physician Paracelsus said, 'The right dose differentiates a poison from a remedy.'

I have seen only two cases of myasthenia in my life, for it is a very rare disease (statistically 15 people in 100,000 develop it), and without medication, patients are totally moribund on a respirator. Muscle atrophy is normal because the more myasthenia patients use their muscles, the worse the fatigue becomes. Patricia, developed myasthenia when she was thirty-one, which was seven years into our marriage. She was expected to die by the time she reached fifty, due to the immune-suppressant drugs she was to take that would lead to an uncontrollable infection.

In Patricia's case, the bean partially cured her, because, in the early days of its use, she was ignorantly overdosed and then, after many years, was able to control the paralysis by wise and experiential administration and reasonable intelligence. She took over from the doctors and medicated herself into usefulness again. By the time we came to London in 1984 at the call of God, she had a permanent silver tracheotomy tube, through which she could breathe and the mucus sucked out in case of a chest infection. And she had a gastrostomy tube through which she ate. When she was fifty-four, both were removed.

A somewhat normal life resumed, and we pioneered HICC starting in 1987. Also, because I had been appointed as bishop of London for Elim, we forged a new relationship between 400 leaders in fifty-four churches in and around the M25, called the Metropolitan Region. Life was busy and full, and we enjoyed the responsibility, involvement, and workload.

However, in 2008, Patricia developed cancer in her right breast. It was controlled by drugs. But in 2010, she also developed triple negative cancer in her left breast and had a lumpectomy. She had thirty days of radiation that appeared to work. But in July 2013, she was found to have a brain tumour that was a metastasis from the breast, and it was suspected endometrial cancer. Water accumulated on the brain. She went into a myasthenic crisis, and her breathing stopped on 11 January 2014. Thus ended the life of a woman of God after forty-seven years of suffering, the last six months intensely.

This thin volume is about suffering, trial, adversity, and God's will, which arose in our home. I watched and experienced it for those forty-seven years. It is simply lifestyle Christianity at its most fluctuating. David the psalmist says, 'Give us help in the hard task,'[6] and that illustrates life as it actually is – the hard task. I asked myself what writings or sermons I had prepared over that length of time regarding those issues in daily life. Had they affected my preaching content? Were the congregations inundated or besieged by teaching that reflected our home conditions? What could I further say about our experience? Hopefully, it would help others.

I write in three ways – HICCBitz, which is a weekly page in our standard handout to the congregation; sermons, which are turned into PowerPoint slides; and spiritual writings, which are a few thoughts on a specific text but are not preached. You will notice the changes as the three are mingled and combined.

But before that opens up, there is time for our first spiritual lesson. The Apostle Paul was like the 'ordeal bean'. But in God's hand, he became a great cure. The great persecutor of the church went about paralysing the early Christians from fear. 'Then Saul, still breathing threats and murder against the disciples of the Lord, went to the high priest, and asked letters from him to the synagogues of Damascus, so that if he found any who were of the Way, whether men or women, he might bring them bound to Jerusalem.'[7]

But when he responded to the heavenly vision and changed from persecution of the church to passion for Christ, his accusers said, 'Is this not he who destroyed those who called on this name [Jesus] in Jerusalem, and has come here for that purpose, so that he might bring them bound to the chief priests?'[8]

Once he was a great and deadly force against the children of the Way. Now he was their supporter and champion. He had switched from being their main enemy to being their closest friend and defender. Like the *éséré* bean, when used wrongly, Paul was quite deadly. Used correctly, he was a cure for the ills of the times. I am sure there are men and women like that in this world. Our prayer is that God will transform their lives and use them for the cure of many distraught souls, changing them from paralysis to productivity.

Chapter 2

The Italian Garden

The Italian Garden was a masterpiece of Victorian planning in Kings Heath Park, Birmingham. My wife and I would often stroll around this small plot of beauty captured by skilled hands and manicured to perfection. It had been one of our courting spots, and now that we were married, it was a peaceful interlude in a busy day. She was in a wheelchair, and I was negotiating it up some brick steps. I was inwardly fuming. Could this possibly be God's will? I should be doing so many other important and vital things, but here was my day restricted and hampered by a sick wife.

At about this time, I had written an article for the *Elim Evangel*, which is now *Direction* magazine. As I was about to finish it my wife walked into my study (she was, at the time, only wheelchair bound when we took outdoor excursions). She looked over my shoulder and said 'You can't leave it like that, 'Make it positive.' So I did.

She taught me a lesson, and I've not forgotten it. At the time that I wrote this article, she had been critically ill for several years. She had suffered much, having been close to death three times. And I was almost overwhelmed and mentally seared by all the suffering. I had taken pen to paper:

> Oh Lord, I'm in distress. In fact, the word to describe my exact feeling is *despair*. I have never sunk so

low and been so disillusioned over circumstances. Everything – yes, literally everything – seems to have gone wrong. The 'working together' of Romans mocks my situation, and God seems to be somewhere beyond an angry sky. I just wait for the next thunderbolt to fall, knowing that the present pain is so great that a little more will not matter. I'm crumbling inside, and all the vain platitudes from fellow saints are the mouthing of cold comfort.

This adversity stretches into the distance in its vastness, and my unbelief pushes it past the horizon. As I open my mouth to sigh, my tongue is parched and dry. 'If only' is my constant theme. I languish in pity so thick that it sticks to my feet in a morass of misery. Words hardly explain my state; they are inadequate to reveal the silent hurt that burns inside.

If I am honest, and honest I must be, I resent this thing called the will of God. I prayed for his hand to lead me into a walk that shines with love's sweet smile, expecting in my zestful hope that he would take me to Transfigurations Mount. Instead, he took me to a valley so dark and drear that even music seemed out of place. Stark trees like dead fingers are my companions and ragged rocks my cold pillow. Here I am hunched in stumbling weariness, slithering on slopes of shale, failing and fussing, moaning and groaning, bleeding and bothered and thoroughly shot through of every personal pride. I lay me down and weep until my soul is dry. Why God, oh why is this the way and not another? Must it be the dark and drear and not the bright and crystal clear? Will this poverty of joy lie like a shadow on my life much longer?

Lord, I cannot stand it. Enough is enough; turn on the lights and speak in the darkness. Change the chaos into peaceful order even if it takes six days, Lord. Begin now and do not leave it. Can I nudge your arm with my tears? Do these broken sighs mean anything to you? Won't you stop as you did to blind Bartimeaus and speak with the voice of victory?

I understand, Lord, that you chasten those whom you love, but the pressure has been on for a long time now. There must be a difference between chastening and this. I'm bruised all over. You've left your mark on my heart and head and I hate to think where else you will lay the stick. Is all this necessary? For I love you; you know that, and I do try to follow you; you know that also. Then why this way which is so alien to all my inclinations and desires?

This was when my wife intervened, and I added this last paragraph:

The psalmist got the victory, so please teach me, Lord. He said, 'I will praise the Lord no matter what happens,'⁹ I don't think that I can. Anyhow, it would take a superhuman effort, and I feel so terribly human at the moment. I've been down twice, and the third time is coming up, and the straws are fast disappearing. But perhaps that may be the answer. I've clutched at too many straws in the past and not at you. Hanging on to the hay can be pretty precarious. I think that I may be getting it, at last, Lord. My grip has been on the transient things that have no substance outside time. It has been all vision and not faith. Because I could not see a way out, I thought there wasn't one. You're getting all the straws sorted out and burning them one by one. It's the heat from the fire that's causing the all the pain. I'm too near the stubble, and I've been reaching into the fire. The sunlight will succeed the shadow, the mountain the valley. While grumbling this matter over with you, I failed to notice the terrain growing smoother, and there is a suggestion of light on the horizon. It's changing, Lord, and I hardly recognised it."

My article was full – well almost (until the end) – of negative selfishness. As I struggled up those steps in the park garden, God suddenly brought it back to mind and stopped me in my tracks. *Think of the benefits, son. Think of the benefits.*

What possible good could come of this situation? I asked myself. Could there be any positives to outweigh the negatives?

Having reached the top step, I walked in silence, pondering what God had said. *Think of the benefits.* Were there *any*? As I looked down at my wife, I suddenly realised that here was an opportunity for conversation – to talk, and laugh, to share intimate moments that only we would understand. It was time for the building of a deeper relationship, a time to draw closer together. That was a benefit. If she had not been in this condition, we would both be doing our thing, miles part, burning up the world; we were both bundles of energy – or had once been!

My peace began to return as I thought of the few moments we were enjoying walking around this beautiful garden. We were sharing the nonsense speech of love that is meaningless to others but, to us very, very precious. The restriction was freedom, freedom to know each other better. It was freedom to share our grief and sorrows, rather than being caught up with the pain of other people – and some were a real pain!

Positivity produces peace – write it large on the wall of your misery. Too many see too little in the current scene. God is out to change us, and he'll do it with or without our permission. We live out our lives in the theatre of life, with angels, demons and sinful men watching. We are the manifold, or multicoloured, wisdom of God, playing out the drama of redemption. Those who watch us want to see God in us; He will often use extreme measures to see we reflect His glory.

Sliding back!

There is a difference between having a formal and a living creed. In the one, we mentally acquiesce to a theory – based on study and revelation. And in the other, we transfer its teaching into action. In other words, we do what we say we believe. We live in the words we speak and become 'doers of the word, and not hearers only'.[10] And we only believe what we actually do!

Backsliding is sliding away from known truth – truth we once lived in. All Christians can go astray like the sheep, the lost coin, and the son; anyone of us can move so far away from God that, like the prodigal son, we become cold of heart. But before the sheep went astray, it was still a sheep. And before the coin was lost it was still a coin. And before the son went astray he was still a son.[11] Once we fail to walk in known truth, we are on a precarious path downwards away from God. Walking in truth is not just holding a formal creed but also living in the living creed. Most formal creeds state that 'where two or three are gathered together there He is in the midst'.[12] Many Christians agree but don't meet, especially in prayer meetings, because they either don't want to meet God, or they do not truly believe it!

This leads me to a time in Patricia's life where she fell away from God, and the circumstances in which she found herself led to that situation. The cause of this backsliding was due to a visit from a leading Anglican minister with a healing ministry who turned up at my house with his entourage while I was at work and, praying for her, pronounced her healed. It was not his standard custom to visit people in their homes, but he'd responded to a request from the wife of the principal of Birmingham Bible Institute, who knew us well. Such was the passion of the request that he felt constrained to do it; in other words, he thought it was right in God's will to do so. However, within a few days, Patricia was admitted to the John Radcliffe Hospital in Oxford, where she had the trachi that she would retain for many years inserted, as her breathing had deteriorated rapidly.

This was the last straw in her sad physical decline. She was already feeding herself through the gastrostomy tube at this point. She was often wheelchair bound. And now, a breathing tube. Life was becoming worse by the year. She stopped reading the Bible and praying and turned away from God. She could not cope with the suffering and God's apparent inaction anymore; her faith had been rocked to its foundations. I, being a minister, could not explain it in spiritual terms that would adequately explain and reconcile adverse circumstances. So I guarded and loved her to bits. That's all I could do.

One day, after many months in this state, she was in the kitchen of our home, and I was at work. She suddenly turned because she felt someone was with her in the room, and she realised it was God. He said in her spirit, *'I'll never leave you or forsake you.'* A few weeks after, that it happened again as she dusted the hallway. And she just sat on the bottom step of the stairs and spoke, 'I suppose you'd better come in again. You're certainly not going to leave me alone.' And with that, she regained her faith, passion, and love for God.

That night as we were in bed, I noticed her Bible again on her bedside table. And when I remarked on it, she told me what had happened. I wept. And I weep now in my memory of that crisis of faith. I had purposefully refrained from remonstrating with her as her pastor on her failure to pursue God, for not praying and reading her Bible, but I had committed her to God and loved her back into spiritual life. I had been patient with her impatience – I had believed for her lack of faith. I could do no more. She was in God's strong hands; they drop nothing!

There is no knowing the depth to which Patricia sank; only God knows. She had been abandoned at the age of three, had lived in six homes by the time she was eleven, and had found God as her father at twelve; here was someone she could trust at last. When she had her trachi, he had, in her estimation, also deserted her. What would you say? I think of Joseph who went from a pit to Potipher's house and then to prison with declining prospects. But in one day he was delivered. So was Patricia. As she grew older, she could look back on the unfortunate episode, and she learnt that God never lets go and dogs our footsteps through life. 'What shall separate us from the love of God?'[13] Nothing – for it is vested in Christ Jesus, and we are engraved on the palms of His hands.

An allegory – God's tattoo: A consolation

'A Maltese man believed to have drowned in the Second World War when his ship was torpedoed in the channel has been found living as a tramp in Sidmouth, Devon.'[14] It was believed that the man had suffered brain damage and amnesia when his ship had sunk and had no clear recollection of what he'd done for the first forty years after the war. His incoherent speech made little sense until someone heard him mention Don Mintoff, the former prime minister of Malta.

'With the help of a British nurse in Malta, a campaign was launched in local newspapers to identify him. Last year Sister Rosina Apploonia, a Maltese nun, wrote to say that he could be her brother, George Borg, believed drowned in 1941.' A tattoo of a cross on his arm he'd had done when he was a young man identified him. After searching through ten layers of clothes, they found it. And so, George, who was seventy-nine would soon be off to Malta with his sister. He had been identified by his tattoo. Little had he realised when it was done that, many years later, it would be a means of recognition and ownership. He would even be unconscious of its presence so accustomed would he be to it.

It may be surprising to many Christians to find that they have been tattooed. When they gave their lives to God by owning Jesus as their Saviour, God owned them, and 'sealed' (tattooed) them with the Holy Spirit of promise. Paul infers that: God has sealed us and given us the Spirit in our hearts as a guarantee.'[15] This sealing means to stamp "with a signet or private mark" for security or preservation. God knows who are His. The process of living may cover up the sign. But underneath, there is and always will be His seal of ownership.

When two young people betroth themselves to each other, they seal their promise with an engagement ring. It's a kind of gold tattoo. It is their pledge to be together forever until one should die. God has betrothed himself to us, for he loves us deeply, and will not let us go. The promise of God is this: 'I give unto them eternal life and they shall never perish.[16] We can walk away from God, but He will never walk away from us. He is in it for life – our life. We may get amnesia, but He can never forget, for in Isaiah 49:16, we read these comforting words – this is God's tattoo engraved by nails on Calvary: 'See, I have inscribed you on the palms of My hands.'[17] He took his hands to heaven when he ascended. That is where he sees the 'travail of His soul'.[18]

Come bombs, torpedoes, or any war manoeuvre against our soul, we will, in the end, be owned before the Father, for we have been sealed. George had ten layers of clothing covering up his tattoo, and we may allow life to encrust God's identification mark, thus hiding from others our ownership. But one day it will be revealed. If he owns us, then he certainly will know, for we are His. We bear the ring (carry the tattoo), we know the love, and we sense the presence. And behind it all, He works for us for our betterment and ultimate blessing. In the midst of trial and adversity, that thought is our strength. It gives confidence amid the swirling tides of doubt when darkness seems to invade our life.

A further allegory – Locusts: An encouragement

Locusts were the plague of American farms for decades, and the locust eruption in the mid-1870s entered into legend. On 6 April 1877, John Pillsbury, the governor of Minnesota, called for a day of prayer to plead for divine deliverance from them. A few days later, the insects rose up and left as inexplicably as they had come, never to return again.

When the Rocky Mountain locusts swarmed, they darkened the skies over vast swathes of the western and central US, from Idaho to Arkansas. One eyewitness said that such a swarm passed over Plattsmouth, Nebraska, in 1875 and was estimated to be 3,000 kilometres (1,800 miles) long and 180 kilometres (108 miles) wide. When the swarm finished feeding, 'You couldn't see that there had ever been a cornfield there,' said one farmer.

These big beefy locusts were considered the greatest threat to agriculture in the West, but the vast swarms vanished a few days after that day of prayer in 1877 and were totally extinct within thirty years. The last recorded one found alive was in 1902 by a river on the Canadian prairie.

Entomologists tried to learn everything they could about this species of locust – what had triggered them to swarm, what they had eaten, and how they reproduced. During that disastrous outbreak in the mid-1880s, farmers fought back with every tool they could muster. When their pioneer wives draped blankets over the produce, the locusts simply ate them and went on with the vegetables. However, when the insects just disappeared, everyone began to ask why.

An ecologist from the University of Wyoming discovered the answer. He and his students recovered 130 intact bodies of the Rocky Mountain Locust, the legacy of the swarm that had risen out of the river valleys of western Wyoming in the early 1600s, long before European settlers changed the face of the West. The analysis of the scattered parts in the ice on Knife Point Glacier confirmed that locust swarms passed regularly over the mountains during the centuries before their extinction.

As he sought further facts, the ecologist came upon the works of Charles Rilley, an entomologist who spent much of the 1870s and 1880s searching for ways to kill the locusts. His conclusion was that ploughing and irrigation would destroy the eggs in their 'permanent breeding zone'. These were in the river valleys of Montana and Wyoming, where the incoming settlers chose to farm. But as less than 10 per cent of the arable land was being cultivated, he doubted if it would have a significant impact.

However, when he superimposed the map of the breeding grounds with the farming map, he found they were identical and that, when the farmers had unwittingly chosen to cultivate the area for wheat and hay in the 1800s, they had inadvertently charted the locusts' extinction. It took thirty years for the prayer of John Pillsbury to be fully answered, but eventually it was, through natural causes.

God can use anything from anyone to answer prayer and will take His own time to accomplish it. Joseph had a vision and no doubt prayed for its fulfilment, but his answer lay in rejection and a dungeon. His brothers sold him into slavery, and his master's wife made false accusations against him. Yet, after seventeen years, God answered the prayer and restored him and, in one day, fulfilled the prophetic dreams he had been given.

It was through an apparent simple happening. Dreams were part of the mystic belief in that age, and the Pharaoh had such an unsettling dream that he demanded interpreters to answer his unease. Joseph could interpret dreams, but little did he realise that answering that mystery would lead to the salvation of his wider family – just like the Montana farmers who, when they cultivated the river valleys, would, in years to come, save their own livelihood and hence their families. God's ways are mysterious and marvellous.

As we go about our lives in the mundane execution of the daily routine, earning an income and living through seasons of life, we can *unsuspectingly* answer our prayers. The faithful servants of Matthew 25 were given various talents to trade. Without knowing or realising it, their lives would change due to the responsibility of the imparted talents, and their reward would be the consequential transformation of their lives. Their faithfulness to the task would unknowingly kill the locusts of dilatoriness, doubt, laziness, fear and self-preservation that could destroy the fruitfulness of life.

The locusts of suffering, adversity, trial, and temptation, which can strip us bare of fruitfulness and denude us of a life harvest, can become just a memory as we extend our trust in the divine pleasure over our lives. Walking in faith, undergirded by omnipotence, we can prevail over circumstances we think are too great, too deep, and too challenging, for *greater* is He that is in us than he that is in the world.

Chapter 3

Pack Up Your Troubles

Britain's war years inspired a front line song favourite that was eventually adopted and adapted by Britian 'Pack Up Your Troubles in Your Old Kit Bag, and Smile, Smile, Smile' written by George Henry Powell and his brother, Felix Powell. Hide your problems and pretend to be happy. Look at the positives, ignore the negatives, and so make it buoyantly through life. Don't be sad, try never to be too serious, and only mourn if you have to. Unfortunately, the same philosophy is often applied to sin. Gloss it over, and it'll be okay!

The structure of most human living – whether by the primitive or sophisticated, the wealthy or the poor, the educated or the ignorant – is based on the seemingly incontrovertible principle that the way to *happiness is having things go your own way.* The world system believes that sidestepping negatives is necessary before the other things can bring cheerfulness. Throughout history, a basic proverb of the world has been that favourable things bring happiness, whereas inauspicious things bring unhappiness. The principle seems so self-evident that most people would not bother to debate it. Yet, godly mourning brings godly happiness, which no amount of human effort or optimistic pretence, based on possibility thinking, can produce. In the routine of ordinary, day-by-day living, the idea of mourning to get happiness seems absurd. But Jesus steps in and confuses the world's maxim.

The epitome of His teaching is paradoxical – seemingly contradictory. What He promises and what He says, seems incongruous or inappropriate and certainly upside down in the eyes of the natural man. The assumed inconsistency of the second biblical beatitude is obvious (for 'beatitude' read blessedness or happiness). What could be more self-contradictory than the idea that the path to happiness is through sadness and that the way to rejoicing is in mourning? 'Blessed are they that mourn, for they shall be comforted.'[19] How can I be happy when the chances are against me?

When we face great sorrow, disappointment, disillusionment, tragedy, or failure, we wish that we could escape them as we escape a thunderstorm by running inside. However, comfort from the troubles of life is much harder to find than shelter from rain. The deeper the sorrow, the harder the pressure, and the worse the despair, the more elusive comfort seems to be. Avoiding pain, trouble, frustration, hardships, and other problems, in the estimation of many, will bring happiness.

The average Christian in this modern age fights against a false sense of assumed piety, which gives the impression that to be religious is to be miserable – how sad and weird! There is also the conjoined error that, to attract people, we must be deliberately upbeat and jolly. But it is this apparent superficiality and slickness that works against us, as it is unintelligent and certainly illusory. Perhaps that is why the church is so unimpressive – in today's climate of spirituality, everything must be kept at a level that fails to produce seriousness and concern over real issues.

The love of God is offered as the answer. He is depicted as one who would never in any way harm us. And that is basically true. It is thought, therefore, that everything should work for our benefit. And so it does, but not in the way we think. As an Arab proverb says, 'All sunshine makes a desert.' There are certain things that only rain will produce; otherwise, the land becomes arid and dry. California seems to have an ideal climate, but it is brown with valley fires for many months.

The real meaning of what Jesus is saying is simply this: Blessed [happy] is the person who is desperately sorry for their own sin and their own unworthiness.[20] That is the meaning of biblical mourning, and the comfort that comes from that tearful confession is the 'peace of God, which surpasses all understanding…[which will] guard your hearts and minds through Christ Jesus.'[21] As another interpretation says, 'You're blessed when you feel you've lost what is most dear to you. Only then can you be embraced by the One most dear to you.'[22] God helps and assists us in losing things that are counterproductive to our spiritual ascent.

This leads us to suspect that sometimes people want Cinderella to be a reality. If only God could wave His magic wand and turn pumpkins into coaches, frogs into horses, rags into gowns, and misery into impossible fulfilment. In our youth, we dreamed upon a star, and magic fluted through a landscape of honey and thistledown, with a sun that never set. Life has now become grey and disappointing. The romance of fairyland has gone.

The words of two sisters echo in time, etched into the fabric of life's cry. 'If you had been here it would not have happened.'[23] Mary and Martha, distraught with sorrow, reproached the Lord, with gentle yet firm blame; he could have done something about the tragedy that had befallen their family. Circumstances had turned for the worse, and Jesus who could change them, hadn't come.

That has been the testimony over many generations, for there is nothing new under heaven. Countless people have been baffled by God's inaction in their circumstances. We did when we ought not to have done, and life changed. We live in a web of needless regrets that tarnishes all we ever do. 'If only!' That plaintive note echoes not only in the morning light. For some, it fills all their years.

Jesus had found joy in that Bethany home, possibly because He was not put under pressure to perform for them His healing or miraculous power. It may be they sought nothing from Him but His friendship, which is a rarity even today. People often manipulate to get things from you. They didn't invite Him to eat in order to soften Him up to win from Him some favour. He found unqualified love and complete acceptance, so much so, that John 11:5 says, 'Now Jesus loved Martha, and her sister, and Lazarus.' Bethany and their house were a haven in the midst of his ministry, and he often would return there.

About Lazarus we know little, except that he died and came back from the dead. Mary broke her alabaster box and anointed the feet of Jesus and was written into the pages of scripture because of her adoration, but Lazarus had no headlines. Yet Jesus loved him. No doubt he would pass in a street unnoticed, and no one would want to interview him. He was just ordinary. But he was special, inasmuch he was loved by Jesus. God loves ordinary people and makes them His friends! 'Therefore his sisters sent unto him, saying, Lord, behold, he whom you love is sick.'[24]

In the world of fairyland, Jesus responds at once, and all is well. But life is not like that. The sisters were grief-stricken when Jesus failed to arrive. We can become like them, when our dreams fail. We wanted the handsome prince to appear and sweep us off our feet, but that kind of make-believe is for children. God does not always respond to our suggestions and commands. Dreams are only fulfilled when God gives them; we cannot build our life on midnight indigestion.

However, Jesus comes, when it seems too late. 'He stinketh',[25] says the Bible. Lazarus was past recovery, and Mary and Martha were mouthing the same words, 'If only...?'

Do we pick up positive or negative things? Who do we talk like? God's inaction rankles humanity, and the human soul wishes that it were different. The promise of God is not to come racing at our bidding, like a servant on call, but to undertake our maturity. As I once heard a preacher say, 'those whom God loves, he beats the hell out of!'

The time of magicians is over, the leprechauns no longer play at the bottom of our garden, and the elfins of make-believe are long since gone! 'When I was a child, I spake as a child, I understood as a child, I thought as a child: but when I became a man, I put away childish things.'[26] The seasons of God are not measured in months and falling leaves, but in the eternal presence. Our Lazaruses may die, and we may never get to the ball, but God promises us something better. The truth is caught in these immortal words: 'A bruised reed shall he not break, and the smoking flax shall he not quench...'[27] We may not be able to turn the clock back by one second and alter what has happened, but God is able to marvellously mend the fuse we have blown. He rectified Eden, and God has never regretted sending His son.

An allegory – Regeneration: A promise in time

A few years back, we visited our twin grandsons in Stoke Newington and went on with them to Clissold Park to play football and eat a little and just to enjoy each other's company and that of my daughter and her husband Steven. We learned as we sat eating that the twins were attending a party in the late afternoon, and they were talking about watching the last episode of *Doctor Who* on BBC television, early evening. Apparently, the previous week's drama had seen the title character regenerating as it closed.

I recalled various newspaper articles during that week as journalists endeavoured to guess who would replace the current actor, David Tennant, as the new Doctor Who. Each time a doctor regenerates, he comes back in a different physical form; and over the years, there had been several new doctors. It was a subtle way of changing actors. However, the BBC put a knowledge embargo on who was to be the new doctor, and so the guessing game began. No one could obtain an inside rumour of who it was, so speculation was rife. But I noticed a small paragraph in one paper that said the BBC might bring David back for two special episodes later in the year, and I realised that he would regenerate in the same form. I didn't tell the boys this; it would spoil their watching and anticipation.

I therefore watched to see what happened and, as I'd thought, the doctor retained the same form, and there was no 'new' doctor. I felt rather smug at having guessed right! Then I switched my thinking to the resurrection of Jesus and to our ultimate resurrection when He returns. When Jesus rose from the dead, He was recognisable; He kept the same form but had a body of different composition.

When Peter protested at the words of Jesus about His death, He called him, with James and John, up the mount,[28] where He was transformed before them. Moses and Elijah also appeared and talked to Jesus about His decease. Thus, there were two witnesses to Peter – James and John – and two witnesses from the Old Testament who spoke of Jesus' death; thus in the mouth of two witnesses[29] shall a thing be established. The three disciples recognised Jesus and also Moses and Elijah,[30] although they had never met the patriarch or the prophet before. There were no photographs, but they knew the history of Israel and transferred written knowledge into visible recognition. The fact that Moses and Elijah were alive showed to the disciples that death was not an end, but the beginning of a new life, vibrant with expectation. When we are changed[31] before or arise after death,[32] at the second coming of our Saviour,[33] we will experience regeneration into a new form. But we will still be recognisable. Mary[34] recognised Jesus in the garden tomb, the two disciples on the Emmaus Road perceived it was Jesus in the breaking of the bread,[35] and Thomas was confronted with a Calvary-marked Christ.[36]

When John saw Jesus on the Isle of Patmos[37] – in the Spirit on the Lord's Day – he saw the resurrected glorified Christ in all His majesty and power, still recognisable but wonderfully changed! That astonishing change can be the portion of each believer in part, as daily he or she sees the reflected glory of Christ by looking into the mirror of the living Word – 'Changed from glory to glory.'[38]

We can be regenerated each day; there will be no flashing lights, sparks, or electricity, but change can come and stay. People will not automatically see any difference. But gradually, over the years, a metamorphosis will occur. People who have not seen you for several years will notice the change, not merely the creases of age but a spiritual essence shining forth.

You'll possess a deeper joy, a finer peace with lasting patience – qualities that can only come from an outside up-surging force, divine in origin – as powerful as or more powerful than mere electricity and stage lights. David Tennant had to be carried into his Tardis for this change to take place, for although he was a fictional time lord, our Jesus is the *Lord of time*,[39] and our transmutation into a spiritual force can take place anywhere and everywhere. Hand in hand with God through all the oscillating variations of trial and trouble, both in the shade and the sun and the flickering half-life of living, we have companionship with eternity itself as He prepares us for otherworldly living. 'And it doth not yet appear what we shall be.'[40]

The stretch marks of pregnancy are a lasting legacy in the flesh of carrying a child to birth. After we built our award-winning church building, someone said to me, 'This building has given you stretch marks.' And the observer was right. Nurturing a dream to fulfilment had left its undeniable mark. No matter how qualified I may have been, and I was well qualified to build it, the stress of finishing it to a high standard, economising on money, and meeting deadlines had been traumatic. The behind-the-scenes practical work and mental combat had been unrelenting. But that is so with most dreams as we strive to fulfil our destiny. In that prospective future, others are caught in the vision but can only live it vicariously, for they were not originally called and must seek to follow another, hoping to gain from them some of the soul-hardening principles of perseverance.

Similarly, looking after my wife and family in the midst of extreme physical suffering had left stretch marks that were undeniable and that could not be expunged. 'A mind that has been stretched will never return to its original dimension.'[41] The pledge to faithfulness 'for better, for worse; for richer, for poorer; and in sickness and in health,' tests one to the ultimate. Watching sickness is often worse than experiencing it. The carer also suffers but in a different manner; it's the vicarious pain of slow death as life ebbs inevitably out. Watching the tide of death invade and then sweep out a loved one leaves the observer jittery with emotional exhaustion.

In the last days of my wife's life, God awoke me at one thirty in the morning. I was instantly awake, with this sentence running through my mind: *Your wife is slowly dying before your eyes.* I reached for my iPad on my desk, on which were several Bible translations which were ready for opening at various passages, so I chose one, supposedly at ransom, but God knew best, and this is what I read: 'A time to be born, and a time to die.'[42] God had spoken and prepared me for the ultimate. The end of forty-seven years of suffering was approaching – stretch marks, of course!

This is why Jesus said, 'Take up thy cross and follow me.'[43] A price has to be met. We live in a society with a soft centre, an easy way out, the skirting of responsibility, liability, and commitment. Our time is precious, and we like squandering it on ourselves. The world tells us we have a right to leisure. But for stretch marks to appear, conception must have taken place. And for that to occur, close relationship must have been established. The seed can then be imparted. The seed of love by association binds one into a faithful response of undying love.

Chapter 4

Teddy Bears

Travelodge, a leading hotel chain, has revealed that it had recently reunited 75,000 teddies with their owners. One of their spokesmen said, 'Interestingly the owners have not just been children; we had a large number of frantic businessmen and women call us regarding their forgotten teddy bear.' And according to Christopher Anderson, a US writer, even Prince Charles travels everywhere with his childhood teddy.

In the 1980s TV series entitled *Brideshead Revisited*, when Sebastian Flyte took his teddy bear to university, it was supposed to be a sign of his eccentricity. But from the statistics just quoted, that may be a longstanding error. It seems apparent that an increasing number of Britons, more than a third of 6,000 people surveyed, keep a soft childhood toy to hug as they sleep, and more than half still have their teddy bear.[44] It is apparent that those who do find it comforting and calming, and it helps them de-stress. About a quarter said the toy reminds them of home whilst away on trips.

As hard as I tried I couldn't remember any teddy I had as a child, and the only 'thing' I took to bed was my wife; I was 25 years old and just married! However, when the children began to arrive, they obviously had teddies. We kept their toys as they passed from childhood to adolescence and then to adulthood. And when they were married, we gave them to their children. As far as I know, all the grandchildren had a teddy except one of my daughter's twins, and he was nearly ten before he decided he wanted one. It sits on a chair next to his bed.

He loved our dog Schmitz, who died a few years ago. So we disinfected and washed his teddy, and gave it to Aubrey to also put on his bedside chair. Whenever anyone visited us at home, Schmitz would race for his teddy (quite a large one), grip it in his mouth, and stand waiting for the visitor, with the expectation he would be relieved of his teddy and told to fetch it when thrown. He was rarely disappointed! Schmitz would often sleep with his head on his teddy like a pillow and seemed to like the gentle comfort it gave.

The advent of the teddy bear toy was in 1902/03 simultaneously in the United States of America and Germany. Toy manufacturers were seeking new models, and in the United States, the bear was named after President Theodore Roosevelt (1901–1909), whose nickname was 'Teddy'. The German one was made by Margarete Steiff, an invalid who developed toys and sent a bear made out of mohair to America. At first it was rejected, but it eventually found favour, and an order was placed for 3,000 from a factory in Giengen, followed soon afterwards with repeat orders as demand swelled.

Thus, around the world, teddies of every kind can be found. Some popular mass-marketed teddy bears made today include Rupert, Sooty, Paddington, and Pudsey Bear. Books have also been written with the teddy bear featured as their main character. These include the Winnie-the-Pooh collections, *Corduroy*, *Teddy Tells Time*, and *Teddy Dressing*. In the foreseeable future, children and adults will go to bed with their favourite teddy; of that there is no doubt.

I do not need to elaborate on what teddy bears stand for in all people's psyches. Stuffed animals bring joy to all children at any time; they go to bed with their teddies for comfort and happy dreams. And so do adults, and their infant cries are usually silenced by the toy. Teddy bears bring smiles to everyone. They typify *comfort*, which is the word that, over the years, has arisen from these facts – teddies give people something to hold and cuddle, and they evoke memories of childhood and home. We all need comfort at some time in our lives, for we are all subject to the vagaries of modern living. Even childhood is fraught with young worries. And at night, as darkness deepens, the small child grips his or soft sewn friend.

However, there are some people who don't need teddies, for they have found the God of all comfort. And in Psalm 23, we read that His 'rod and staff comfort me [us]'. The word *comfort* here means 'to sigh with'. Sometimes we cannot speak, for there are no words suitable – no word that can give meaning – in the midst of trial. So we just sigh with the person – which is all that is needed, if the person sighing is God. We find this same notion in the words of Boaz in the Old Testament book of Ruth. Boaz, speaking kindly to Ruth, 'comforted her'. Since my salvation, I take God to bed with me every night. He is a comfort like none other. 'What a wonderful God we have—the one who so wonderfully comforts and strengthens us in our hardships and trials.'[45]

A hymn comes to mind:

There's within my heart a melody
Jesus whispers sweet and low:
Fear not, I am with thee, peace, be still
in all of life's ebb and flow.
Jesus, Jesus, Jesus,
sweetest name I know,
fills my every longing,
keeps me singing as I go.[46]

For those who cannot remember that old hymn, or have forgoten it, or never knew it, there is a tendency to look back in nastolgia, for the past often appears better than it was. But the bible tells us not to do that because we clutch at misinterpreted shadows. History reviewed can be misunderstood and exaggerated. 'Do not say, "Why were the old days better than these?" For it is not wise to ask such questions.'[47] Even as a baby gains comfort from a coddling blanket or teddy bear, so we gain consolation from nostalgia, reaching into the past to make the present liveable. We tend to look back because the foreground is shadowy and uncertain, and we are ignorant of God's intended purposes. Often we cannot discern the divine will for our lives, and the past beckons with some speculative assurance of immediate comfort.

We must also remember that we were younger when that history was written. Our maturity would have been partially formed and our understanding limited by self-perception; and it is possible that our commitment would have been compromised by human weakness. Therefore, the Ecclesiastes writer states 'do not say' that the old days were better. For, if we do so, our mouth may sink our future, and our retrospective yearnings may compromise our current joy, howbeit sullied by doubt.

Looking back can have merits but also misfortune, and often, the latter outweighs the former. Lot's wife looked back and became what she should have been – *salt*! She longed for the sin pots of Sodom, for to her, these could not have been better years, but doing so destroyed her. Israel, in growing discontent, looked back. And it cost God's chosen people forty years of privation, trial, and suffering – for Egypt was their prison, not their freedom.

Examples of faith

The Bible is full of people who responded well to adversity and those who also fared poorly. These, *we must* consider; looking at them is wise and instructive. The Holy Spirit's selected history is there to warn and prepare us for the pilgrim way – so that we can avoid shipwreck of our souls after walking many years with God. The five-fold opposition common to humanity will daunt our steps on the upward way. Difficulties, distress, discouragement, delay, and temptations are accompaniments of the way.

History has recorded the tales of these adventurers in faith – who were confronted with almost insurmountable barriers to faith – from every sphere. They were pioneers in the midst of adversity and show us that we are mistaken if we think action is all that is required of saints in the war waged against them; in addition to attacking, they must bear, forbear, and withstand. There must be courage and patience in perseverance. 'That you may not be sluggish, but imitators of those who through faith and patience inherit the promises.'[48]

My wife stood at the window of our breakfast room with her Bible open on the windowsill, looking out to our beautiful garden and also looking at an uncertain future. She was praying that she might live long enough to see our children reach adulthood. She looked down and read, 'You shall live until your hair is white.'[49] I noticed one week before she died that her hair had turned white. She died. God kept his word. She saw not only her children reach adulthood but our grandchildren as well. It is said that God will give us bread and water, but sometimes we get duck and green peas!

Wasteful wishing

Wishing for the past can stifle the future, for we dwell on what could have been and not what the present can become. In a time of unbearable crisis, we look back and believe it was better then. But the sunlight of that escaping day may not have brought us to maturity. Thus we defend ourselves with memories as sheets of armour rather than use our present crisis to win varied honours of our profession.

We must contend a little and wait, while delay is vivified by hope and expectation. It is the sunshine in stormy times, the streaked light on darkened horizons. Our problem today is that the glare of the sacrificial fire blinds and scares us, shrivelling our manifest profession unlike martyrs of old, who sealed their faith with blood. Basically, we tend to distrust God's absolute sufficiency.

It is human to be dispirited and afraid of an unknown future and a difficult present, so that we long for those times in past days of apparent unfading joy. If heaven had no martyrs, it would have no earnest endurance. And unless we likewise are willing to forsake all for His sake, we cannot prove His keeping power. Jesus set His face towards the Cross and cast an indelible pattern. Often, modern theology escapes that well-trodden route, excusing the hard-won lessons of a rough and uneven way.

God's absolute sufficiency can only be tested in those dim times of uncertainty, when there is cold and not heat, rain and not sunshine. The seasons conspire to prove God. The inducement to walk that blood-sprinkled way is that *God is for us* – to magnify the vastness of the task, the greatness of the prize, and the nobility of the witness. Israel saw the grapes but tasted not the vintage because the giants stood as high as the topmost blossom. They forgot the Red Sea. Even when confronted with those grapes of Eschol, Israel doubted; the largest grapes always appear to grow in the shade of the tallest giants!

If we must look back, we should fix our eyes on the right focal point. The promised people looked past their deliverance to their first environment – garlic, leeks, and onions, the foodstuff of slavery. The grapes are ours bequeathed by God; the vintage is our draft of joy. Let not the grapes fail on the vine or be eaten by another. Fight for the future; it is full of prospective splendour. They that honour God He will honour. And if we care to believe that He is all sufficient, then He will be. Our trust will prove him. God is not only *for* us and *with* us, He is also *within* us.[50] Emmanuel is our security – 'God with us' – but we know that, since Calvary, he is now within us. He was, therefore, with us when we were twenty-five years old, when we were eighty-five, and throughout every decade in between and has lived through the circumstances of our history. So how can one decade be better than another when God is in control?

An allegory – Video Nasties: God's MRI

'The body of a killer who was executed a few years ago in Texas was recently released as a three-dimensional computer image that will become a medical teaching aid . . . this digital body can be viewed in any plane and fully dissected on computer.'[51] The US National Library of Medicine, using his corpse, had just completed this 'Visible Human Project' – that is, a digital reproduction of the killer's body. He had left his remains to science. And after his execution by lethal injection, they were flown to the University of Colorado Health Sciences Center, where they were subjected to a variety of computer-controlled scans. His remains were then encased in gelatine, frozen, and sliced into 1,870 one-millimetre sections, which were digitally photographed and stored with the rest of the computerised data.

Such an undertaking seems gruesome, but it is necessary for scientists and medical practitioners' pursuit of knowledge. In this visual application to the furtherance of knowledge, researchers still cannot find a person's mind, soul, or spirit. They can investigate as many sections as they like. They will not find out how man thinks, how he reacts to emotional stimuli, and how he worships.

The writer of Ecclesiastes says, 'As you do not know the path of the wind, or how the body is formed in a mother's womb, so you cannot understand the work of God, the Maker of all things.'[52] Mankind is a curiously wrought work of God, and man will forever be labouring to understand the greatest miracle of God's creation. Scientists can look whichever way they want at a human body, but only God knows the heart, the seat of our life. 'My substance was not hid from you, when I was made in secret,'[53] says the shepherd king. God was doing an ultrasonic scan long before the doctors. The real you and me are hidden from television cameras. They can dissect us into even smaller units than one millimetre apiece, but all they will find is tissue and skin. Our inwardness, or the secret parts of our personality and spiritual perception, are a mystery and will remain so, but not to God.

Even as the minute body sections of Joseph Jernigan are studied rigorously to learn the function of the various parts, God so studies our motives, attitudes, desires, and aspirations. The only difference is that He does it while we are alive. His study is painless but thorough. We may leave our body to science, but it is far better to leave our soul to God. Jesus said on the Cross, 'Into your hands I commend my spirit.'[54] His spirit was safe in God's hand. He drops nothing except our sins. He has His video of our hearts but erases all scenes when we ask forgiveness. The video library on our life has only one tape in it. It portrays us kneeling at the penitent seat, asking for His pardon. That's where it starts, and after that, it's blank. It is used as a teaching aid for other sinners. God is saying, 'Come to me, and I will give you rest', something the doctors cannot do. Just look at the video. There is nothing on it. You are free, free at last! It says more by being blank than it would if it were crammed with information.

Overview of the Church

John sees Jesus standing in heaven. It is the only picture of Him in the New Testament scripture. There are seven stars in His right hand, which represent the seven churches in Turkey. He addresses each specifically, portraying His own special attributes in contrast to thiers. And then He sets out to correct their lack, for they are in need of renewal. He has given them a scan and knows the situation.

The body of the church has come under His scrutiny. It was not frozen in gelatine or cut into myriad pieces, but He knows as no one knows: 'And his eyes penetrated like flames of fire.'[55] God's eyes are His electronic microscope. No one and nothing can avoid the discernment of that divine glance. As He sits as the Ancient of Days, Daniel the prophet saw him in a vision and describes the infant of Bethlehem: 'His body was like chrysolite, his face like lightning, his eyes like flaming torches, his arms and legs like the gleam of burnished bronze, and his voice like the sound of a multitude.'[56]

Among the oldest writing in scripture is a verse that confirms that God can judge us: 'Does he not see my ways and count my every step?'[57]And David, the sweet psalmist, echoes the words from personal experience 'All my longings lie open before you, O Lord; my sighing is not hidden from you.'[58] Pleasures, pain, perplexities, and permissiveness are all known and recorded. Jesus saw Nathaniel under a fig tree and knew he would be a fruitful man. He saw Peter fishing and knew he would be a foundation.[59] He saw, looking up into a tree, small Zacchaeus and knew he would be a giant in generosity.[60] He called for a woman's husband and knew she had had five and was living with a sixth.[61] She met the seventh, even Jesus.

He can see us amid our trial and understand the vexation of spirit as pain throbs in the midnight hour – knows completely how we fare and what is troubling us. The enforced ache of celibacy through sickness that disturbs sanctity, the privation of peace -- and the restless chaos as we fight for self-control are all open to His gaze, and there is no condemnation at all. His love exceeds our pitiful response to suffering. His faithfulness outruns our doubting, and His mercy assuages our fears. His MRI scan reveals all situations perfectly, and He always makes the right diagnosis! His eyelids try the children of man for they never close. But in our weakness, he not only sees but speaks in His own inimitable way to alleviate the discomfort.

Chapter 5

The Nawab of Pataudi

The Nawab of Pataudi died at seventy but can be remembered for his cricketing ability. His aim was to be a supreme batsman. But in 1961, as a passenger in a car, his right eye was pierced by a shard of glass from the windscreen, which made it difficult for him to judge the bowling length, especially against spinners. Immediately, he set out to rebuild his career and, four months later, captained the Indian Board President's XI against Ted Dexter's MCC team at Hyderabad.

He found that, when he went in to bat, he saw two balls about 150 millimetres apart, so he decided to hit the nearest one – and reached 35. But then, he took out the contact lens and kept his bad eye closed and reached 70. Four months later, he made his Test debut for India against England in Delhi and made 13, 64, 32, and 103 in his first four innings. His record obviously begs the question as to what he might have been or achieved – perhaps he could have been one of the greatest batsman ever.

When at Winchester in 1954, he was known as a cricketing prodigy. During his four years in the school XI, he scored 2,956 runs at an overall average of 56.85. And when the captain scored 1,068 runs in the season, he beat the record set by Douglas Jardine, England's eventual captain. He reached his peak in 1961 while at Oxford. By the end of June, nearly at the end of the academic year, with three games to play, he was only 92 runs short of his father's record when the accident occurred. When Yorkshire, which was then the greatest county side, played Oxford, he scored 106 and 103 respectively and 131 against Cambridge.

Looking back on his cricketing life after the accident, he wrote, 'I have concentrated on trying to make myself a useful one [batsman] and a better fielder than my father.'[62] He did what he could, not what he couldn't; recognised his enforced physical disability; and made as much of what he could with what was left. Even so, during his later life, with only one eye, he scored 203 not out against England in Deli and 128 not out against Australia in Madras – an amazing feat. Many other world players couldn't do that with two eyes!

Rather than bemoan his inability because of physical disadvantage, the Nawab concentrated on what he could do and got on with it. What magnificent courage and determination. Being useful is better than not being at all. It is said of scriptural Mary, who broke into a man's meeting with an alabaster box of perfume to anoint Jesus; 'She did what she could.'[63] She could weep, wipe, and worship; what more did she need to do? Our problem is that we don't do what we can, and we blame others, including God, for our lack. One eye or two, do what you can. Don't sit and mope.

I've had the privilege of watching my wife master a rare neurone muscular disease for over forty-seven years, without complaining or blaming anyone for her condition. She has surmounted extreme difficulties, even the loss of one eye through a botched operation, and she has watched as others have protested inability, running rings around them. At her best, she was probably less physically able to do what she did than others would be. But she did it because that's the nature of determination and commitment – of an inner spirit that ascends the impossible and does what it can, and does it well. Being useful is not as good as being brilliant, but it's better than sitting around and slouching in discontent. Look at the positives, I always say. Look at the positives.

Making fifty runs is not as good as making a hundred, but it's better than making none! Performing at a lower level is better than not performing at all. Modern sociology, in its distorted wisdom, will sanction a school sports day but not make children enrol in its competition because they may lose. But real wisdom says you 'must' enrol, even if you do lose. Doing will soon mature you and make you better able to cope in life, because we cannot win at everything.

Life is usually a question of win/lose or lose/lose and very rarely win/win. If you can't cope with losing a 100-metre dash race, how will you handle being rejected at a job interview?

By being 'useful', the Nawab gave pleasure to an innumerable company of people because even his 'useful' was better than many peoples' best. Don't downgrade or underestimate yourself. Make do with your current ability. It may bless a multitude. We may not surpass the dream. But just live the dream. And help others as you help yourself. Therefore, we must consider further the biblical command, for command it is: 'In the day of prosperity be joyful, but in the day of adversity consider: Surely God has appointed the one as well as the other.'[64]

One morning, I met an old woman with an equally old dog in the local park, and both were grumpy. Her dog was even more so because my dog was jumping about the field thinking this was playtime. The Alsatian was too old, had arthritis, and was too poor tempered to respond other than to simply snarl and snap, unable to catch Schmitz. The old woman looked as if she's was snarling as she tried to fend him off. I stood as Schmitz moved off, realising that there was no fun here. So he sniffed around as I stood speaking about incidentals.

As we spoke, a woman strode past in a bright pink coat and with a clopperty-clop of her high wedge-shaped heels. Inevitably, it had been raining the night before, and the parkland was sodden and covered in pools of water that were draining across the path into the river about three metres to my left. It wasn't very deep, just a few millimetres, but sufficient for her to pause.

As she did, I called after her, 'Do you want me to lay my coat down?'

'Oh no,' she replied.

'How about if I carry you across then?' I said.

'*Could* you?' she replied. And I wasn't sure if that was a question as to my strength or her weight!

However, the decision made, she stepped onto the grass, which seemed drier, and immediately sank in mud up to the top of her heels. She struggled to get back on the path, used the water that was flowing over it to wash away the dirt – didn't make a very good job of it – and strode off. I looked at the grumpy woman, and she looked at me. And with that knowing look of the years and the sagacity born of living, we both said, 'She should have kept to the path.' And we went on our way knowing we had the answer to living!

As I did so, the Lord just quietly spoke to my heart and said, *If she had kept on the pathway, the water would have washed her soles. When troubles come across your path like water, you try and sidestep to miss it but find yourself in greater trouble. It is always best to walk straight on, for I have designed the depth and the flow, and it is always more beneficial to keep on, rather than divert. In passing through, you'll simply wash your soul, for my trials are designed to purify.*

Hand of adversity

Two men were thrown into the sea just 200 yards from shore on the North Devon coast when their fourteen-foot boat sank in a notorious stretch known as Hartland Races. After trying to swim against the currents, they were swept out two miles from the coast. One of them drowned, but the other, Leighton Jeffery, was rescued. The coxswain of the Appledore lifeboat said, 'We saw what looked like a buoy, but the man managed to hold a hand out of the water, and because it was white from the cold, our searchlight picked it up.'[65] He had been in the water twelve hours and was at the limit of life expectancy. In effect, *his adversity* saved him.

Bob Wilson, the former England goalkeeper, wrote a book entitled *Behind the Network: My Autobiography*. It reveals how the footballer overcame tragedy in his life and rose a whole person. His two brothers were killed in the war. His oldest brother was shot down in a Spitfire in 1942; he was just nineteen. And Billy, who was a rear gunner, was killed in action in a Lancaster a year later. Later in life, Wilson also lost his thirty-one-year-old daughter to a rare type of cancer. He remarks that another famous goalkeeper has aptly summed up his painful journey: 'In the mist of winter I finally learned that there was within me an invincible summer.'[66] He reveals a rich and strong life, not lost in perpetual grief.

Adversity, trials and opposition may come, but how we deal with them proves life. It is often that, out of adversity, strength arises, and a ministry is born. It was on a programme from the Glass Cathedral, Garden Grove, California that I heard and saw a young boy of just over four years with a very rare disease that had been diagnosed too late for remedy. He could die of a heart attack at any moment, as his cardiovascular system had been affected. His mother was the choir leader of all the young children in the church, and she and her husband just glowed with God's love.

The boy had recently been in hospital as an emergency for nine days and was watching his heartbeat on a monitor. He asked his mother what it was, and she said, 'The blimps show your heart's beating.'

'What happens if it stops?' he asked.

'Well, you go to see Jesus,' his mother told him.

His reply was a classic, 'Whoopee.'

He later sang a song and requested no clapping. One line of that song was, "I'm a promise, and I'm full of potentiality."

Some people can look at the bright side of any adverse situation. Instead of grumbling, they are full of grace. Actually, to us Christians, problems should be the stepping stones to greater maturity, not a slew of despondency, which they so often are. Frances Bacon said, 'Prosperity doth best discover vice, but adversity doth best discover virtue.' This is an echo of the Apostle Paul's words: 'We continue to shout our praise even when we're hemmed in with troubles, because we know how troubles can develop passionate patience in us, and how that patience in turn forges the tempered steel of virtue.'[67]

I once had a treadmill exercise test to determine the state of my heart. I went through various stages, increasing speed and elevation, and eventuality it was stopped and the results analysed. The doctor said, 'You have an enlarged heart.'

There was a momentary flicker of panic, but then he assured me that this was good. It simply proved I had been an athlete in my youth. It wasn't just my athletic youth; having bought and converted six homes – throwing about sacks of cement, barrowing numerous quantities of sand, lifting heavy loads, and labouring at all trades – I had caused my heart to enlarge and increase its oxygen capacity. It was similar to increasing your biceps or six-pack!

What had been a stress situation – hard training and hard labour – had worked to my advantage. I had grown inside, and that is what problems do in everyday life. We do not welcome them, but we do have an inner strength that comes to our rescue. An iron in the soul that presses out against that which is pressing in – a rigid resistance to hostile conditions – is not so much an inner condition but the resident Spirit of Jesus. When you compare His suffering and ours, there is such a differential that His overshadows ours with such intensity that we wonder why we complain. Paul says, 'For momentary, light affliction is producing for us an eternal weight of glory'[68] – these small potatoes, as one translation put it!

Therefore consider

'In the day of prosperity be joyful, but in the day of adversity consider: Surely God has appointed the one as well as the other.'[69] This cry applies to most Christians, for cares can corrode us, fears dismay us, and disappointments confound us. In our relationships, there are the seeds of bereavement. In our possessions reside the elements of danger. And in our affections are traces of anxious torment. We are tempted, at times, to cry with Lamentations, 'I am the man who has seen affliction by the rod of his wrath,'[70] and, 'Is it nothing to you, all you that pass by? Behold, and see if there be any sorrow like unto my sorrow."[71] But to do so would be singularly self-important ignorance and arrogance, for there is 'no temptation which has overtaken you except such as is common to man.'[72] But one does wonder, if God is

37

our friend, why does he not exempt us from such trials? And if He is our father, why does he not protect his child? The eternal question is this: *If I am His, why am I thus?*

Peter, addressing the early church, said we are 'elect according to the foreknowledge of God the Father'.[73] But he also said, 'Beloved, do not think it strange concerning the fiery trial which is to try you, as though some strange thing happened to you.'[74] The first compensates and consoles for the second. Religion does not *exempt* us from the evil day, but it does *prepare* us for it. And within the host of biblical instructions and examples, not the least is our text – 'in the day of adversity consider'. Talking to His disciples, Jesus said, 'In the world you will have tribulation.'[75] And King David inferred, 'Many are the afflictions of the righteous, but the LORD delivers him out of them all.'[76] So both the Old and New Testament confirm the rightness and certainty of trial and tribulation.

However, our calling is 'reasonable service',[77] not unjust and callous but destined for glory. God is the author of every good thing, and our pilgrimage to Him is by our effort – for we are not carried, but we are guided. He works *within us* to form His Majesty enabling us to *walk in worthiness*. It is, therefore, realistic for us to consider that our religion is sensible. And like saints of old, we can say, 'I thought on my ways and turned my feet to His testimonies.'[78] This word extends to all parts of religion. Thus in the midst of adversity, we can say confidently, 'If God be for us, who can be against us?'[79] His testimonies are sure and shot through with divine love and affection. Thus, we should consider Him in all aspects, especially when it comes to His ways in our life. The Bible says, 'Consider Him.'[80] And so we will. His design for us must, therefore, be perfect.

As the words of this hymn promise that we can find comfort in giving ourselves to Him and to His perfect design:

O love that wilt not let me go,
I rest my weary soul in Thee;
I give Thee back the life I owe,

That in Thine ocean depths its flow
May richer, fuller be.[81]

Let us consider just our duty

Our text says, 'God has appointed the one as well as the other.'[82] It is God's sovereign will, 'Therefore humble yourselves under the mighty hand of God, that He may exalt you in due time, casting all your care upon Him, for He cares for you.'[83] Samuel knew about this, "And Samuel told him [Eli] every whit, and hid nothing from him. And he said, It is the LORD: let him do what seems to him good."[84]

The lessons of adversity are fourfold – correction, prevention, instruction, and usefulness. The last one was prominent among Puritan writers; life must *always* be useful or effective! The purpose of our life here must be productivity. And in that fruitfulness, we must consider men of old and their faring with God. We may be under grace, but Jesus came to fulfil the law! His basic dealing with men does not change from generation to generation. Abraham committed sin in taking Hagar, and now we have the Middles East crisis because of Ishmael. He forgave the transgression but did not remove the problem.

The state of the heart must outweigh the conduct of the life. Therefore, John said, 'You have left your first love',[85] a gross sin indeed. Thus the sin of omission was recognised and revealed; often tribulation reveals the heart's condition. There are common laws that suggest that, if we do one thing, another will automatically happen. So we thus teach our children that *normal retribution follows waywardness.* Hear God's parental heart as He speaks: 'O Ephraim, what shall I do unto thee? O Judah, what shall I do unto thee? For your goodness is as a morning cloud, and as the early dew it goeth away.'[86] Knowing He must do something, He struggles to manifest love in their error. It is the same for all earthly fathers who love their children. Love demands a correction to ensure future compliance and a path towards improvement. God loves us too much to leave us alone. Job says it right: 'Behold, God will not cast away a perfect man.'[87] His attempt is to bring us to perfection in the daily swirl of life, for we 'are being transformed into the same image from glory to glory, just as by the Spirit of the Lord.'[88]

The subtly of backsliding is often ignored as we talk of the sins of commission. Proverbs comes to our aid: 'The backslider in heart will be filled with his own ways.'[89] And as long as we walk in our way, we are backsliding. Do not be surprised if correction comes. Although there is no apparent decrease in fervour, what formality can arise in our hearts, what decay of devotion, and what coldness of love? We need to pray with the Old Testament saints: 'I will not offend any more: That which I see not teach thou me: if I have done iniquity, I will do no more.'[90]

Let this be our prayer:

Burn fire of God! By Thine own love transcending
Let all I hold be Thine, and Thine alone!
Heart, mind and will, a sacrifice ascending,
Consumed by fire from out Thy fiery Throne.[91] (italics added)

Chapter 6

Vibration in Tansit

The poultry industry loses £8 million each year due to cracked eggshells. As a means to cure this problem, the Eggss Authority sponsored the development of an electronic wonder egg, made of transparent Perspex, which will light up when subjected to shocks that would crack a normal egg. It was then used to show where, in the hen-to-distributor process, the eggs suffer the severest vibrations sufficient to break them.

We are like those eggshells, often broken in transit, just one shock too many. The vibrations of life cause our victory to vanish. Knowing our susceptibilities to such accidents, Jesus came and travelled our shadow-splashed route from the cradle to the tomb. He, like us, experienced the unevenness of the path. He knows where the roughest places are. And for Him, Calvary was the worst of all. There is no point on our journey where He has not been. He came to where we were, becoming bone of our bone and flesh of our flesh. The scripture says that it became Him to become a man. What could naked divinity clothe itself with to make it better than it was? The crinkled flesh of humanity can often be improved by a subtle weave, but God needs no such help. His voluntarily took man's frail form.

Jesus wore flesh!

He fitted himself with tissue and skin, and the Bible says it suited him. In fact, 'It Became Him.'[92] Christ's original dress was not the seamless robe but a sinless human body that shone through the linen with a light of radiant holiness. We wear clothes, but He wore flesh and gave it the dignity that Adam lost. God's long suffering took on a new shade of mercy when Jesus was born. Humanity listened to the prophet's voice and heard that God loved them, but when that Evangel took feet and hands and walked among the sighs of men and touched their hearts and hurts, then they saw that God was real. Jesus was God in action. He is the *word* walking – along our road.

Jesus shows us His downward mobility from heaven to earth, to the cross, to the grave, and to the skies. Charles Wesley wrote a hymn explaining as only he could about Jesus' self-emptying, noting that He 'Emptied Himself of all but love, and bled for Adam's helpless race!' After the resurrection, Jesus stood on the lake shore and made breakfast for the toiling disciples. I believe that, if you want to be great, you should learn to cook breakfast!

Cavett Robert wrote, 'If we study the lives of great men and women carefully and unemotionally we find that, invariably, greatness was developed, tested and revealed through the darker periods of their lives. One of the largest tributaries of the River of Greatness is always the Stream of Adversity.' If we run from trial, we run from greatness. Life in all its vicissitudes makes us what we are. Humble subservience through pain is the answer.

Joining hands

The mystery of the incarnation is too far beyond our understanding; the gulf is as wide as an insect and a star. It is as if a beetle could know the heartache of a human and a fly could perceive the pining of a man. God joined hands across the chasm between flesh and spirit and connected heaven and earth in reconciliation. God turned His eye to the tear of earth and Christ 'became' that we might sit with God. Jesus abased Himself that he might abound towards us in stunning love. The Bible says He is above us, among us, for us, and one of us. Trials and triumphs – he knows them all: Oh the ecstasy of being human and walking with God!

He was born to minister and to give His life as a ransom for many. To do that, He took the fabric of flesh. They tore it on cruel Calvary. Blood and water flowed out. Jesus was shaken by the tough hands of injustice, and His brow furrowed like a sea-grooved shore. His back was laid bare to the ploughshares of demented punishment. Those carpenters' hands were spiked with timber pegs. His feet were pierced with a wooden nail. That worldwide heart was punctured – by a soldier's spear but first by the absence of His father.

In all that man could do, it was but the shell, the husk, the outer flesh that was broken. The yoke, the kernel, the inner spirit – what of that? His was not merely human suffering but spiritual anguish. 'He knew no sin was made sin for us that might be made the righteousness of God in Him.'[93] By taking all our sins, He deserved to die. He became the chief of sinners, though He was the King of Righteousness. It was the Father's will to make His Son perfect through suffering. He was jolted along the rough road of life until, in Gethsemane, His head was marked with perspiring blood. 'Can you drink my cup?'[94] This was His question to the eager disciples. No one could, for in that vessel was the breaking of every man, the burden of every soul, and the shadow of the darkest hour.

All the king's horses!

Jesus was not an experiment to save costs but the embodiment of love for this lost world of humanity. He 'became' that we might become sons of God.[95] He was made like unto His brethren, in all points tempted. But in all points, He was triumphant. He was crated up with humanity as they jostled against Him in the hubbub of life.

He proved that God can do what 'all the king's men' could not do. And that is, put us 'together again' – so much together that we could possess the land of delight and live in the fullness. Our 'egg life' might get severely jostled, but He has been that way. He has left us a legacy of Zion's land, a term for a unique possession all our own, tailored to our needs. In spiritual language there is a possession that God had consigned for us all called 'the Land.' When reach and occupy this land, it will be for us – that best portion suited to our needs and requirements.

This parable is a means of understanding God and His direction in our lives. If we can relate spiritual truth to practical terms, we will have a better understanding of what is required of us and what God has designed for those who love Him. If we are to live down here the life that God wants for us and that we want to have, then His teaching must become our identity. Escapism that longs for the third heaven must be moderated by a significant appreciation of the moods and manner of life in the Spirit. The 'today' of our Christian experience and its splendour, should be shot through with the *thoroughfares of Glory* as we travel to our Canaan, making the vibrations en route to 'the Land' the experience of our redemption.

Unfortunately, many are the preachers who wax eloquent about positive thinking and teach that anybody can reach limitless prospects; all it takes is a constructive mind or attitude. But many people also live with shattered dreams. This is one of life's major traumas. For these people, life did not turn out as expected or wanted, and the consequence is a life of disillusionment. Sadness undergirds their lives, and they seem never to rise above mediocrity; their hopes are dashed against a seeming wall of adverse circumstances. Single people long for a relationship, and married people, for a fulfilment not yet experienced within the marriage bond.

Unhappiness bleeds through all facets of society. And if the truth were known (and often it isn't) in the average church, there are many disappointed people who find it hard to reconcile their faith to their circumstances; somehow their current faith belies their present environment. I am sure many of us pastors are out of touch with reality in our sermons, and we often fail to touch the real hearts of people in their daily dismay. Perhaps we are too glib about the faith and its recompense. And because we don't have answers, we hide this 'lack' within theological rhetoric that is meaningless. It was H. G. Wells who said, 'The secret splendour of our intentions and the poverty of our achievements.'[96] The disparity often confounds and withers us.

Mark Twain said, 'Seldom does an individual exceed his own expectations.' And perhaps that is the underlying basis of living. Most of us expect reward out of life because we strive for it. And general opinion holds that there must be a universal law that, if we do, we shall. Life is, therefore, cruel if it does not hear and see what we do and withholds a just recompense for diligence. There seems to be a certain right of inheritance that is propounded for good works, healthy thoughts, and good attitudes. But the criminals get rich!

Joseph had a dream, and therefore, the general rule is that everybody else ought to have one. There were eleven brothers who didn't. And they sarcastically said, *'Look, this dreamer is coming!'*[97] And dreamer Joseph was. But it took many years for that dream to come to fruition. The time between the dream and it becoming reality was fraught with betrayal, disappointment, deprivation, baseless accusation, and incarceration. Joseph's feet were bound in iron so he could feed a multitude. His total subjugation emphasised his elevation to peerage, and his hostile environment is minimised. But it is the intimidating background that is the springboard to the heights.

The secret of God's dream, and we should be very careful to prove he did give it, is that it will eventually 'come to pass'. But we often forget that 'obstacles are those frightful things you see when you take your eyes off your goals' [Henry Ford]. God is an expert at delay, for while we wait, we mature so that we can handle the reward. If the fulfilment is too early it could kill us off. Unfortunately, too often our lives often correspond to our convictions. It is a question of *our whims* or *His will*. His will took Jacob to Haran for twenty years, Moses to the backside of the desert of forty years. And Jesus had to wait eighteen years before he could start his ministry. The dark seasons of the soul are more to do with our inability to focus on God's timing than on actual inability to perform.

One golden rule when walking God's way and towards his purpose is to ensure we are not too comfortable. We must rid ourselves of the protection that comes from the blight of security. Society with a glut of charity will stifle dreams. Most Christian parents spoil their children for they over-provide. God is good at cutting the umbilical cord. 'You need to keep on patiently doing God's will if you want him to do for you all that he has promised.'[98] God is also good at famines! 'Wherefore glorify the LORD *in the fires*'[99] [Italics mine].

A lady who had a pain in her side went to her doctor; he said that she had appendicitis and needed an operation. She decided to get a second opinion from another doctor, who said she had heart problems. She said, 'I'm going back to my first doctor. I'd rather have appendicitis than heart problems.' We know as we age that sometimes we don't always get 'good news' from our doctors. But we cannot change the diagnosis; only God can. That is the crux of life. We have to accept what is served us, like it or not. It is how we accept the situation, not the situation that defines us. The situation cannot often be changed, but how we react can.

It is clear that many Christians do not have answers to imponderable problems, especially those related to the sickness and death of a loved one. Therefore, words are inadequate, so why speak them? We speak probably because of a compulsion to identity with suffering through Christian compassion and an urge to express sympathy. We are creatures of the heart and long to help, if only we could. But we can't, and there it must stay. There is a locked-up frenzy in our inner self that cries out in anguish to know. Yet knowing does not bring light; it only brings a greater burden.

Look at Job surrounded by *friends*, who reminisce with him and yet chide him for misunderstanding God. But they are limited by ignorance of God's will. God's will is often like a tennis ball that can be hit anywhere so that it can land where we want it. But it may not be God's will, just a tennis racket wielded skilfully but in error. Our frustrations, temptations, unhappiness, and sin can lead us out of God's will because of self-determination. This cannot be God, not for me. He loves me too much. And so He does. *But* the night continues!

We can glibly quote oft-used texts, like, 'All things work together for good.' And possibly they do. But time may not reveal that, for eternity is God's domain. Eternity is where we are heading, and we often confuse the substance of time for the ultimate reality when it isn't. Humanity has become stranded in time and its procurements, which simultaneously both dazzle and dim Zion's joy and settled peace. We walk through a troubled, turbulent landscape trying to find a vantage point for direction, and we spy a Cross that points the way. The Cross answers most things; it certainly explains the love of God.

So we suffer by degrees and compare ourselves to the blessed master, who suffered more than all – suffered for the joy that was set before him: 'Looking unto Jesus, the author and finisher of our faith, who *for the joy that was set before Him* endured the Cross, despising the shame, and has sat down at the right hand of the throne of God.'[100] [Italics mine]. The joy that is set before guaranteed the sitting down – not just anywhere, but in eternity's throne, which straddles time and timeless existence. For the Cross perfected Him.

In this world is variety, change, and succession; it does not alter. We bathe in the light, which is soon enveloped by darkness. We rejoice in the spring flush and see it wane into summer, which is overtaken by the riot of autumn, only to be submersed by the rains and frost of winter. The cycles come and go. Equally chequered is the variety of human life. Our circumstances change, and in that diversity, we see the glory of God's providence. As Reverend William Jay said, 'Providence is God rendering natural events subservient to spiritual purposes.' I doubt it can be better put. God has a plan. He will bring it to fruition. The world will frown and smile upon us in varying degrees, and it is that juxtaposition that troubles us. Like the disciples, we say, 'It is good for us to be here.' And God says, 'Arise. Let us go hence.' And so we do, and we find maturity in the valley. That's the way. That's the blessed life.

An allegory – Gritting our teeth: Saved by two millimetres

However, the Egyptians, the persecutors of Israel, probably seemed the most miserable people on earth, not through personal trials – although they may have had those – because it is reputed that the reason the pharaohs never smiled was because their teeth were bad. Judith Miller, a dental surgeon turned Egyptologist has said that there were no dentists in ancient Egypt, except those who gave potions or recited spells. Her exhaustive work that covered 4,000 years has revealed that there is no trace of dental work during this period. To prove her theory, she examined over 500 skulls and jaws from the Duckworth Osteological Collection at the University of Cambridge and Natural History Museum in London.

Amenhotep II was one of Egypt's greatest pharaohs, who ruled when the Egyptians were at their most powerful, peaceful, and fabulously wealthy. He built temples and raised statues to Gods to be remembered. And he was, but not for those feats; he was remembered for his bad teeth. On examination of his mummy, it was found that Amenhotep's teeth were in a terrible condition and that he must have endured considerable pain over many years; each mouthful would have been agony.

It is surprising that given Egypt boasted skilled physicians and advanced knowledge of anatomy, they never dealt with the peoples' tooth decay. Many suffered the ravages of dental disease most of their lives, and many died as a result. And the rest had to grin or grimace and bear it. Miller found that most people had lost at least one tooth, and those that were left were riddled with cavities and worn to stumps. This condition led to abscesses and either loss of bone in the jaw or a chronic infection of the bone and blood poisoning.

It seems that the greatest destroyer was physical wear brought on by the food they ate. It flattened the cusps and stripped off the enamel, thus eroding the soft dentine beneath. This damage was bad enough, but they also suffered from cavities, which begins when carbohydrate residues build up on the teeth to form plaque, which is colonised by bacteria in the mouth. This bacteria releases acid that attacks the enamel and dentine and forms cavities.

The Egyptian diet was rich and varied, and it was noticed that, around 4000 BC, people started settling along the banks of Nile and took up agriculture, switching their diet to one rich in carbohydrates. They grew barley and emmer wheat to make beer and bread, and it seems that was the problem. On analysis, it was found that the bread was usually contaminated with grit – fine grains ground off the millstone. Also sand blown in because it was baked outdoors. They also failed to remove the fibrous husks, with the result that the bread was grainy and gritty and quickly wore down the teeth to the pulp. The emmer flour is sticky and would cling, and as they failed to clean their teeth, it soon accumulated around the base of the teeth, pushing down the gum line and causing rot.

It seems that Job knew a thing or two about decaying teeth. 'My bone clings to my skin and to my flesh, and I have escaped by the skin of my teeth.'[101] His trouble continued until he was down to the point of losing his teeth and his life when God intervened. We are not sure if his local chemist ran out of toothbrushes or toothpaste, or whether he ate emmer wheat. But Job certainly knew the pain of decaying teeth and the faith-testing will of God. In Job 2:13 it is recorded thus, 'So they sat down with him on the ground seven days and seven nights, and no one spoke a word to him, for they saw that his grief was very great.' Numb from the shock and dumb from the suffering, he was so afflicted he was hanging on by the skin of his teeth. He further says, 'When I go to bed I think, 'Oh, that it were morning,' and then I toss [agitated restlessness] till dawn.' [102] In all of us is there is the toss and tumble as we work our way to triumph. It is part and parcel of life in the multitude of vexing vagaries. Our bed sheets may indeed cover our body, but what covers the mind? For, the mind throws off any form of wrap that brings comfort.

God allowed Satan to interfere with Job's life to test his faith. And when Job was at death's door, God reversed the process. How thin is the skin (enamel) of a tooth? Perhaps less than two millimetres? And that was the stage at which God appeared? Many trials we come into are God's will for our growth. There is a philosophy that teaches that Christians can escape *all* trials, tribulations, and enemy attacks. The purveyors of this philosophy obviously haven't read their Bible.

'Wherefore glorify ye the LORD in the fires.'[103] And so we must, for we are to manifest His glory in all aspects of our life – spiritual, natural, and civil – including suffering. No portion or part is to be excluded – the whole man for the whole Lord. Especially as our text infers *in the fires*. And what fires we have. No one is exempt. Fire is a figurative biblical symbol for trials and tribulations, and so is water on occasions. 'We went through fire and through water: but you brought us out into a wealthy place.'[104] And 'When you pass through the waters, I will be with you; and through the rivers, they shall not overflow you. When you walk through the fire, you shall not be burned, nor shall the flame scorch you.'[105] There is no doubt we will pass through. But there is always the other side. The New Testament echoes this promise: 'Beloved, do not think it strange concerning the fiery trial which is to try you, as though some strange thing happened to you.'[106] As the ancient sage speaks, 'For affliction does not come from the dust, nor does trouble spring from the ground; *yet man is born to trouble*, as the sparks fly upward.'[107][Emphasis mine].

As Christians, we are guaranteed suffering: 'Many are the afflictions of *the righteous*, but the LORD delivers him out of them all.'[108] And why should we find this strange? Is it because we expect heaven's favourite to be the inheritor of untold and manifold blessings? It seems logical that the Father's love would bestow upon Jesus all mercies, yet he suffered more than us all. 'Though He was a Son, yet He learned obedience by the things which He suffered. And having been perfected, He became the author of eternal salvation…'[109] Thus, there must be conformity between the head and the members: 'And He is the head of the body, the church.'[110] As he is, so are we. We cannot be partial and choose the best bits. Life in the spirit in its entirety is our blessing! God does not expect us to be more than but, rather, like our master in all things. We cannot exceed Him, but we must follow Him. He was 'a man of sorrows and acquainted with grief'.[111] And perhaps there is a lesson there?

'For whom the Lord loves He chastens, and scourges every son whom He receives',[112] especially Joseph. Consider therefore these divine words: 'As many as I love, I rebuke and chasten.'[113] This is not suitable language in the modern church, where any cleric would hesitate to rebuke anyone over anything, lest they leave the sanctuary. Many Chrsitians are not in submission to delegated legal authority and are also flippant with the judge of all the earth. They harden themselves by infidel reasoning and stoical apathy. The only course is to cry to the one who 'gives songs in the night.'[114] Thus, 'I will look to the Lord; I will wait for the God of my salvation; my God will hear me.'[115] And we must exclaim further, 'From the end of the earth I will cry to You, when my heart is overwhelmed; lead me to the rock that is higher than I."[116]

Thus, it is our duty to 'show forth Your [His] praise'.[117] And if we don't, the very stones would cry out.[118] As sheep of His pasture, we are identified, branded, and also inspired to be like the shepherd. 'But you are a chosen generation, a royal priesthood, a holy nation, His own special people, that you may proclaim the praises of Him who called you out of darkness into His marvellous light.'[119] We show forth His praise by our language and life, and we exhibit this when we confirm His will that nothing comes to pass by chance. Irrespective of what happens, whether pleasant or painful, God is in it. And he said, 'The Lord gave, and the Lord has taken away; blessed be the name of the Lord.'[120] We are full tilt in gratitude when we acknowledge this overriding purpose of God.

We should also realise that 'The Lord is righteous in all His ways, gracious in all His works.'[121] Because of this divine rectitude, we should be careful not to indulge our criticism of Him and ensure no blame is placed on his shoulders – that he is free from censure. As his children, we have been punished far less than our sins deserve. So we can voice with David, 'I know, O Lord, that Your judgments are right, and that in faithfulness You have afflicted me.' [122] The Lord is just in His sovereignty towards us. He shows His love by pruning us into fruitfulness; the tree he does not want he does not touch. The pruning shears and sharp spade informs us we are loved beyond measure.

God can correct us whilst we are in transit, because He knows all things past, current, and future. He is a threefold God, in charge of history, time, and eternity. He knows our defects and maladies, which He can rectify in any place and at any time. And He does not err in His continuance, for He is good towards us. It is from this goodness that comes the mollifying comfort for every sorrow wrung from the breaking heart. It is a good father who imposes restraints to teach the child, a good husbandman who mulches and prunes to save the tree; God does no less to ensure our perfection. 'Furthermore we have had fathers of our flesh which corrected us, and we gave them reverence: shall we not much rather be in subjection unto the Father of spirits, and live? For they verily for a few days chastened us after their own pleasure; but he for our profit, that we might be partakers of his holiness.'[123] Profit and holiness are conjoined and complement and support each other.

All these 'things' that came and come upon us are for our wisdom, humility, and tender-heartedness and to make us spiritually minded. Against such, there is no law. They are intended to wean us from the earth and make us fit for heaven. We lose things, but we don't lose all. It could be far worse, and it isn't. We have the promises of scripture and the sympathy of friends. Therefore the words *fear not* ring in the darkness and shout from Genesis to Revelation, for the Bible is replete with positive promises. 'Is anything too hard for the Lord?'[124] He raises the dead and makes a way where there is no way. Joseph and David both witnessed His almighty power. So did Daniel in the lion's den and Elijah in the famine.

The age of miracles has not passed. 'Jesus Christ is the same yesterday, and today, and for ever.'[125] He is as near to us as he was to the patriarchs of old. Abraham 'staggered not at the promise of God through unbelief; but was strong in faith, giving glory to God.'[126] We, unfortunately, may not be so fervent or believing. We may be more like the Old Testament people of God, who 'limited the Holy One of Israel'.[127] However, in spite of wayward Israel, there were times that he called to mind the greatness of his sovereignty. 'And I said, this is my infirmity: but I will remember the years of the right hand of the most High.'[128] This passage recalls faithful, forgiving, and fulfilling years with God in the sanctuary and triumphant on the battlefield.

So we each, with the passing years, have *opportunity* to witness. We have that privilege. It will convince the sceptic, encourage the languid, and convict the sinner. The weak are strengthened, the doubting transformed, and the mournful enlivened. We can illustrate the principles of faith, recommend the advantages of religion, and exemplify the master we serve. Scripture tells us, 'For in him we live, and move, and have our being.' [129] So we ought to demonstrate that and make the scriptures as real as God himself. In our 'uprising' and our 'down-sitting'[130] he is there, never to leave us or to forsake us.

It is said to prospective clerics that the title of a sermon should contain 80 per cent of their preparation time. And in our lives, we should often look back at the title of our lives, and remember its conviction and strategy. What are our lives actually saying to those who look on? Could we even give a title for the life so far lived? Or is there nothing on the book cover? What do I want people to see and read in the daily motions of my being? A young woman came to Jesus, and he said, 'She has done what she could.'[131] What she could do was worship, and that was enough. Perhaps that could be the title of her new life, as she was lifted from an unsavoury lifestyle into that of a princess with God.

Thus, we can declare *hope* for the future and peace for the present. This is based on the fact that, in weakness, we are made strong. 'But he said to me, "My grace is sufficient for you, for my power is made perfect in weakness." Therefore I will boast all the more gladly about my weaknesses, so that Christ's power may rest on me. That is why, for Christ's sake, I delight in weaknesses.'[132] In the steps of the master, we echo Isaiah's prophetic cry: 'Surely he took up our *infirmities* and carried our *sorrows*, yet we considered him *stricken* by God, *smitten* by him, and *afflicted*. But he was *pierced* for our transgressions; he was *crushed* for our iniquities.'[133] Here is the sevenfold suffering of the Saviour in our stead. He looked for a harvest; we, likewise, the dying seed, yield a fruitful field.[134] [Italcs added to emphasise Chrsit's severfold suffering].

Chapter 7

If Cows Could Fly

Your way was in the sea and your paths in the mighty
waters, and your footprints may not be known.
—Psalm 77:19

With a shrug of exasperation you hear someone say, 'Yes, and if cows could fly' – meaning, of course, that *it* (whatever it is) will never happen is. Yet, 'In April 1999, a Japanese fishing boat sank after a cow fell on it from a clear sky. Investigators alleged that Russian soldiers had commandeered an army plane for a bit of rustling, but had opened the rear doors when the cow grew agitated.'[135] It was not so much blessings but bovine from heaven! I presume that most of us would get somewhat perturbed if, after praying for God's best, a side of beef scuttled us.

I also assume that any insurance investigator would raise more than just an eyebrow at that account of that disaster. 'Honest, judge, a cow hit me from heaven!' Titters round the courtroom. I don't suppose the sailors thought it was funny. I'm sure the cow didn't. Any reasonable person would assume that mad cow disease had already started. 'Pull the other one,' I can hear someone say, or, 'Pull all four if it comes to that!'

Where is this leading? Well, to the fact that things happen in life that are unexpected and entirely unbelievable. Such a case exists in the New Testament. 'Now Peter continued knocking; and when they opened the door and saw him, they were astonished.'[136] The disciples had *prayed* that God would set him free from prison, and He did. It was unexpected and entirely unbelievable; after all they had just prayed!

When God answers our prayers, we are often thrown into silence because the response was unexpected and entirely unbelievable. We know that God can answer our prayers, but we don't believe He will. Our belief is that God loves us but not that much. Miracles are for others and the first-century church. We live in the culture of the twentieth century. What is reasonable is possible. Cows falling from heaven are not reasonable and, therefore, not expectable.

There is a text that states, 'I can do all things through Christ who strengthens me.'[137] It is greatly misunderstood. For instance, I might wish I was an opera singer. But even in Christ that is not a possibility. Or I might want to win the Formula 1 driving championship or play cricket for England, both impossibilities, no matter how much I trust in Christ and pray for His intervention. Glib preachers resort to this text in their positive preaching, which brings bondage to many people. *We can only excel at that which we are destined to fulfil.*

The psalmist said, 'And [He] strengthened me with strength in my soul.'[138] The word *strength* means to blow within or upon. Hence, the strength of the balloon is dependent upon it being limp enough to receive the breath. In the limpness of my weakness is the opportunity for God to work and fill me with His strengthening Spirit. We must be prepared to be shapeless enough for God to use. But remember that a balloon will expand according to its original predesigned shape. The breath inside determines its final contour, but only according to its manufactured restraints. *God knows our predesigned shape.* It is best to leave our destiny to Him. But always call on the breath of the Holy Spirit to fill us to that maximum, so we will reach our ultimate profile.

Our concept of victory is through strength, but God's is through weakness. The scripture and the song say, 'Let the weak say, I am strong.'[139] We are sacramental elements in the hands of the Lord and, as such, need to understand the value of brokenness. It has been said that we are not here to 'deepen our own spiritual life, but [to] be broken for Jesus' sake.'[140] The Japanese often break vases and mend them with golden glue, making the vessel more valuable because of the remedial work and skill of the craftsman! God is the finest craftsman.

Grapes must be crushed to yield wine, and soldiers die for victory to be achieved. No man who enlists expects anything else than to fall on the field of battle; to anticipate anything else is to join under false pretences! The purpose of God in all His dealings with us is to make our concept of Jesus Christ greater than our experience. We are often too concerned with how we stand on the ladder of achievement, rather than with knowing Him.

He thus brings us into the deep waters so that we will cast our eyes away to Him and learn the strength of weakness. The beginning of John's gospel reinforces this. 'In the beginning was the Word, and the Word was with God, and the Word was God...and the Word was made FLESH.' Could there be any weakness greater than this? But in this limited ability came supreme victory. Jacob's strength was crippled so that he could learn that, in weakness, he could become Israel.[141] God's power is often vested in vessels that the world would count fit for the scrap heap. *God has to fight the current of our own strength* when we are ready to be discarded because of inability; then He performs the miracle.

Natural effort

Malcolm Gladwell, who has authored a book entitled *The Tipping Point*, states that, 'The greatest athletes, entrepreneurs, musicians and scientists emerge only after spending at least three hours a day for a decade mastering their chosen field.'[142] It appears that the minimum amount of time that a person needs to spend to reach the pinnacle of greatness is 10,000 hours.

This obsessive approach is normal in many people, Jonny Wilkinson of rugby fame, who kicked the winning drop goal against

Australia in the 2003 Rugby World Cup final, and the Williams' sisters at tennis, to name a few. Victoria Pendleton, who won gold in Beijing, trained for four hours a day, six days a week for four years. Rebecca Adlington, who won two gold medals at the same Olympics, trained for 8,840 hours from the age of twelve. Maxim Vengerov, one of the world's greatest violinists, started training at four years of age when given a small fiddle and displayed remarkable aptitude. He practised seven hours a day, from when his mother returned from work at eight in the evening and then taught him until four o'clock in the morning.

If God is there for us, why do we have to exert so much effort and labour to excel? Well, it is clear that, to gain anything of value, earnest effort must be expended with constant endeavour to duty. Nothing of value is cheaply earned. I know that, in a rough calculation, I have spent, over the last decade, well over 10,000 hours preparing PowerPoint sermons.

So what of our text, "I can do all things . . ." can we fit into that promise for promise? Common sense tells us that we cannot do everything because we are not built to succeed at everything we touch. We just don't have the aptitude, so we must always gauge God's will and follow His specific guidance. It is then that we can do 'all things', but mostly through overcoming the distresses of life. The vicissitudes in the *variety of sufferings* and *our response to apparent misfortune* is the main thrust of Paul's arguments.

Paul is not speaking of healing or riches or of succeeding in the world by ability or gift; he is talking about his life of provision and penury. He also says: 'For I have learned how to get along happily whether I have much or little. I know how to live on almost nothing or with everything. I have learned the secret of contentment in every situation, whether it be a full stomach or hunger, plenty or want; for I can do everything God asks me to with the help of Christ who gives me the strength and power.'[143] Paul does not ask the impossible! He only does what God asks him to do. Our problem is that we self-impose good works on ourselves and blame God if we fail. Our problems in life are often self-prepared.

God does not promise to heal everybody; he didn't heal Paul, although Paul besought God to do so three times.[144] As we look into the book of Acts, we see a lame man[145] accosting Peter and John as they walked into the temple, a man Jesus passed by many times but did not heal – then. When Jesus sat before his father on the hillside, after ministering successfully to the crowd, the disciples wrestled against the storm on the lake, and he just stayed and watched and did nothing until four o'clock in the morning.[146] There are certain things God does not do. And so in our extremity, he may not talk but leave us to sail the storm. But in him we can reach above *all things – we can reach harbour!*[147]

In these cases of disruptive trial and opposition – when changing phases or conditions prevail against us, when money is plentiful and also sparse, when we are in rude health or health that is suspect and failing – it is possible to do 'all things' allowable in Christ. An inner iron arises that presses out against the pressures working their way in. And we have an overcoming experience – thus doing *all things*, in God's permitted will, we become victors.

An allegory – Unnecessary penance: Hair shirts

Sir Thomas More was born in Milk Street, London, on 7 February 1478, son of Sir John More, a prominent judge. He was educated at St Anthony's School in London. As a youth, he served as a page in the household of Archbishop Morton, who anticipated More would become a 'marvellous man.' Thomas More went on to study at Oxford under Thomas Linacre and William Grocyn.

Around 1494, he returned to London to study law, was admitted to Lincoln's Inn in 1496, and became a barrister in 1501. Yet More did not automatically follow in his father's footsteps. He was torn between a monastic calling and a life of civil service. While at Lincoln's Inn, he determined to become a monk and subjected himself to the discipline of the Carthusians, living at a nearby monastery and taking part *in* the monastic life. The prayer, fasting, and penance habits stayed with him for the rest of his life. He wore a hair shirt next to his skin.

More's desire for monasticism was finally overcome by his sense of duty to serve his country in the field of politics. He entered Parliament in 1504 and married for the first time in 1504 or 1505. He was convicted of treason and beheaded in 1535. On his death, it was found he still wore a hair shirt full of lice next to his skin. It seems his early monastic calling had pursued him all his life thereafter.

It seems that our repeated vows are very much like More's hair shirt and are certainly full of lice. A self-imposed penance is mistakenly believed to earn favour with God. To do without and to bear uncomfortable conditions is viewed, misguidedly, as an act that somehow appeases God. At the beginning of each year, we pledge to ourselves, with our eyes on God for approval, to undertake a remedial process of living. In the majority of cases, those kinds of vows fade after a short time. Although the intention is firm, the flesh is weak.

The fact that we make these promises shows we are not happy with our lifestyle. There is something wanting in our view of ourselves. Pressures from the world convince us we need to adjust our lifestyle to fit the criteria of what is expected of a committed Christian. In other words, we come to believe we need to justify our priesthood and please God. We can never please God by our efforts. Rather, we please Him by our humility and total dependence on Him. For in Him, we move and have our being. If it were possible to justify ourselves by works, there would have been no need for Christ to be crucified. It might be wise to consider what kind of lice shirt we are wearing in our daily attempt at placating God. Our chosen hair shirts can take many forms. Encoded in human kind is a desire to please God and to earn His favour. But in Christ, we already have it.

The Word of God says we are 'a chosen generation, a royal priesthood, a holy nation, His own special people, that you may proclaim the praises of Him who called you out of darkness into His marvellous light.'[148] Such a catalogue of renown should fill us with confidence to approach his throne, undimmed by personal self-afflicted penance. 'Let us therefore come boldly to the throne of grace that we may obtain mercy and find grace to help in time of need.'[149] Don't drag your heels. Rather, stride forward into the divine and awesome presence, knowing He is not only monarch of eternity but also loving father of our life.

The way

Humanity can control many things but not the sea. The sea is irrepressible and in a state of ceaseless change; it is an element that is notoriously unpredictable. We may sail across its wild swells and be lashed by its foaming waves, but we will never be its master; there is always the perfect storm. Similarly, it seems that, in this world, we are surrounded by wild alarms – tempestuous scenes of life, convulsions of opposition, and relentless fluctuations –creating alarm and uncertainty. Our one consolation is that God rules supreme over everything. It is that thought, and only that thought, that brings serenity.

The courtiers of King Canute flattered him into believing that his word was immutable and that he was so powerful that he could even command the tide to recede. But when he placed his throne amid the incoming waves, he almost drowned as he made his escape. The only thing man can do is swim in the sea or voyage upon it. He can neither stay its fury nor command its peace. It almost seems as if the waves show us sufferance and, once in a while, reveal their absolute fury with terrible proof of their uncontrollable power.

However, 'God's way in the sea is mighty.'[150] At his word, it became a wall, allowing passage into freedom for his homeless people and then crashing with relentless force, annihilating Egypt's glory. In a different dispensation, He commanded the sea to be still and the winds to cease their fury; they made their obeisance at His word. He who had control over the denizens of the deep ordered one of its inhabitants to apprehend and carry a disobedient prophet to his destiny, and another became his treasurer, supplying his tribute money.

The furious elements

If we speak of God's way being in the sea, *we must see far more than that*. There are, upon this earth, elements that are uncontrollable and changeable – elements that cause us continual angst. Invisible evil spiritual forces that are beyond our comprehension surround us daily. Politics suborn our peace by repetitious avarice, and complexities of interpersonal relationships strain our sanity with the violence of self-will. We struggle to reach the maturity we want in God and to fulfil our destiny, feeling thwarted by myriad circumstances that combine to spoil our intended goal.

In this upheaval of those furious elements, God has his hook in their noses and a bridle in their mouths – he leads; they follow. He allows or permits by his greatness; they come so far and no farther. He controls and rules where humankind cannot, and He dictates where man can only mouth vacuous words. When we feel like a rudderless boat or a withered windblown autumn leaf, we know in our inner mind that 'It is well with our soul.'[151] When we contemplate the agitations of world powers, the confusion of political ambitions, and the gathering portentions of evil, we are directed to our duty. 'In your patience possess you your souls.'[152]

We know that there is one who can release and bind at a word, whose *way* is in the sea. Whatever the fury released upon us in whatever form and in whatever situation, we believe that God will not only intervene but also limit the danger and destruction – permitting, controlling, or overruling. It is enough for us to know that His purposes will come to fruition. 'Surely the wrath of men shall praise thee; the residue of wrath you will gird upon thee.'[153]

Human life and spiritual agency

As God's children, we are not exempt from the gathering storms. And like countless others, we find ourselves toiling in the waves, waiting for Jesus to appear. The wind is contrary, and we are tossed up and down, to and fro, seeming to be in jeopardy. But we know

He can say 'Peace. Be still', and it will be so. It requires great faith to stay calm when we feel ourselves drifting with the current and sense that our anchor has dragged free.

Yet there is calmness because we are convinced of security; *He permits but also at the same time overrules.* We watch the sea thundering upon the shores of our island empire and know that there is a limit. It will not swallow the land; the tide will come up only so far and no further because God has planned it so. The waves rush in their fury and yet break and fall in disarray, covering themselves with angry white foam. We turn and walk away, knowing all is well; another tide has come and turned.

'His way is in the sea', and we must learn from that, that He is more than able to be in the midst of our adversaries whatever their form may be. Jesus, speaking to Pilate, said, 'You would have no power over me if it were not given to you from above.'[154] In the spiritual realm, God reigns. And without His consent, nothing would be. We view daily change knowing that, like the sea, not one droplet remains still. Even as the sea is consant in motion and aggravated by contrary winds, so our soul responds to that constant process of change. And in that varying progression of life; in those shifting scenes, He is ever present. God is in it all. 'When the enemy shall come in like a flood, the Spirit of the LORD shall lift up a standard against him.'[155]

Paths of glory

Superseding the frightening crash and vibration of the waves, the Lord's *way* is in the sea. But also His 'path is in great waters.'[156] This means there is a direct route through the heaving contorting mass. Paths are directional; it means a fixed and definite plan. *God is not haphazard; he navigates the sea.* There are no visible pointers or roads on the ocean. A captain must use his compass and the stars. God is acting with a predetermined plan in view; he knows it like a captain knows their charts. *He is working out one purpose with many acts.* His own honour demands that this is so, for he will bring 'many sons to glory'.[157]

We should not worry if we cannot trace the path, for scripture says, 'His footsteps are not known."[158] We can be confident in the knowledge that he is acting on our behalf, not because we see footprints in the way. For in certain seasons, we must 'walk by faith not by sight'.[159] We also tend to miss the footsteps of God in the meandering multifarious avenues of life. We cannot understand how often *this* means *that*. We think our prayers are not answered, when God has granted us his favour; we misread and mistake Him. Never forget that *His way* is in the sea; it solves many problems we find difficult to understand. 'For momentary, light affliction is producing for us an eternal weight of glory far beyond all comparison...'[160] But that mindset is not human but divine – to ensure we live heaven on earth. We need to put on the whole armour of God; our mind must be set on God, for Satan will fire upon us constantly to cause doubt in God.

An allegory – 'Bulletproof priest': The armour of God

One of the first successful bulletproof vests was designed and manufactured by a young Polish priest, Cashimir Zeglan. And having heard some sermons, I would say that for certain ministers, such a vest would be the best form of clerical dress!

Zeglan's interest was aroused when, on 28 October 1893, the mayor of Chicago, Carter Harrison, was shot. Harrison was taking a well-earned rest after he had given an address at the world's fair, when Eugene Prendergast, a crank police officer, burst into his mansion and shot him. As the local clergy tried to make some sense of the tragedy, Zeglan's thoughts turned to ways of preventing gunshot wounds and, in particular, the wearing of appropriately reinforced clothing.

The year of 1893 was a popular time for new ideas about bulletproof garments. A San Francisco gang pulled off a jewel heist wearing armour made of baseball catcher's padding reinforced with boilerplates. The armour was so bulky that gangsters had to back into the horse-drawn escape carriage. Both sides of the Atlantic rang out with gunshots aimed at apparently bulletproof entertainers, but eventually they fell silent as the phase passed.

However, when young Cashimir was not gainfully carrying out his duties at St Stanislaus Kosta Church, he experimented with all sorts of materials in pursuing his development. Using hair, steel shavings, and clumps of moss, he continued his experiments. Basically, he was trying to dissipate the kinetic energy from a relatively small area as the bullet pierced the skin into a wider area. He tried various materials criss-crossed in their weave to form a strong net and included steel plates. After several years and after having visited some master weavers in Vienna, in June 1897, Zeglan announced he had solved the problem. On a sweltering June evening, in the lecture hall of the Chicago College of Dentistry, Zeglan brought forth his cloth, and Count Zarnecki, an Austrian army officer using a .44 calibre revolver, fired thirty bullets into the material. All were stopped.

The secret lay in the use of silk used by Japanese samurai, including a 1.6-millimetre-thick steel plate.

Zeglan eventually put his invention to the ultimate test and wore such a garment himself on the stage of Manhattan's Koster & Bial's Music Hall, with the condition that he was not to be shot in the face. Count Zarnecki obliged his friend and shot him at point-blank range. All Zeglan felt was a slight 'tap,' and it was all over, and he was proved right.

They say that one of the prerequisite qualities for entering the ministry is to be thick-skinned – in effect, to wear a bulletproof cassock. To be in charge is to invite militant criticism; it goes with the job. You cannot please all the people all the time. Neither would one want to; attempting to do so could lead to compromise. One of the 'blessings' of leadership is the ability to withstand opposition and to pick the bullets out of the vest later on.

People who aim for leadership fail to appreciate the need for personal protection against Christians and the devil. Sometimes our greatest opposition comes from within the church, not from the world outside. Often, the congregation for the most part, are disinterested in the church and its workings. And, changing the metaphor, it is the little foxes of small-mindedness that cause the most problems.

Sadly to say, I have come across many traditional religious snipers who seem to delight in using ministers for target practice. When I was regional superintendent of the Metropolitan Region, I was called to sort out personal squabbles at a leadership level. It necessitated spiking the guns and encouraging the ministers to wear bulletproof vests – the righteousness of Christ.

There is an absorption factor that one can develop in Christ that spreads the kinetic energy of criticism. As we dwell in the power of Calvary's Cross we experience death to our feelings and ambitions (that are outside of Christ's will). And we are able to stop the bullets in their trajectory, thereby nullifying them and ensuring they have little or no effect. Perhaps we are left with a little bruising!

Dead men can't feel. Pain is assuaged in the silk weave of grace and stainless steel mixture of Christ's forgiving love, which when woven together can stop any projectile. The five factors of mental distress are solved. Hurry, worry, flurry, fear, and faces are bidden depart; in fact they cannot pierce the armour.

Chapter 8

Tommy Gun

*Joseph is a fruitful bough, a fruitful bough by a
well; his branches run over the wall.*
—Genesis 49:22

I have one significant memory of childhood Christmas, which was
opening some presents from my Uncle Eric when I was about eight
years of age. I have no other advent memories of my childhood that
are of any import. There is a block in remembering anything else,
and no doubt some psychologist would be able to pinpoint some
serious disorder. However, it could be that I was so contented that
there is nothing of any moment worth remembering. Or maybe it
was so boring I blotted it out entirely. Or perhaps, I simply have a
bad memory; that is always a possibility.

That momentous day I do remember, I was given a fort called St
Michael and some lead soldiers, both of which Eric had made, and
they were excellently crafted. He also included a Tommy gun with a
crated wheel and clapper, which allowed the gun to sound very much
like the original – well, for childhood imagination it could!

It is possible that because it was homemade, and a great deal of
effort and skill went into it, I remembered it as a labour of love. It
also may be that it was one of the most expensive presents I had ever
had; at this time in our family life, money was in short supply, as it

was with many in our neighbourhood. We didn't expect much for Christmas, and what little we received was very much appreciated.

It is not without some significance that, eight years later, I also became a pattern maker like Uncle Eric. I had a natural aptitude for practical work with my hands – woodwork and drawing specifically. It seemed, therefore, sensible to work in an industry where these talents could be proficiently used. However, I often wonder if that Christmas present set in motion a desire to emulate my uncle and produce beautiful handcrafted goods.

We never really know what influences us as we make our choices. However, I don't believe life is haphazard. I believe God has all things in control. Just before my youngest son sat his O levels, he contracted an infection that virtually closed his eyes. They were so swollen he could not read and was admitted to hospital. He still passed the ten subjects, having taken mathematics a year early, and went on to be a doctor. And I wonder if that spell in hospital influenced his future life?

My first wife wanted to be a missionary nurse and sent off her letter. But the reply calling her for an interview was delivered while she was at work and was put on the sideboard by her mother. It slipped down the back and was discovered many years later. If she had read it and responded, she might not have married me. And had she gone it would have been the time of the massacres by the African uprising. I believe that Christmas presents, a spell in hospital, and a lost letter all had significance. God guides us, by way of natural events, towards profound life choices and His order.

What we count as accidents, chance, or luck may be God in the shadows. I have seen too much to dismiss God out of the apparent common and luckless misfortune. I know he can turn anything to His and our advantage. We often mither about life's happenings as if God hasn't the wit or the ability to overrule or counter the situation, but the scriptures and our personal experience prove that God is in control.

God can retrieve situations: Turning things around

The history revealed in the Bible shows that God can retrieve people and situations from all kinds of predicaments. The black pits of calamity can become the sun-tinged vales of fruitfulness. God has a plan; nothing can thwart it. Extreme cases of adversity can be resolved in a surprising manner by God, who is constantly inexplicable. God is not confined by normal parameters but supersedes the obvious constraints of situations. The prophetic word given to Joseph was fulfilled in the process of God's time. The route was circuitous and winding, but eventually, it led to the dream becoming reality – the picture became a film. When God's hand is with a person, it will deliver him or her to his or her destiny. The bottle thrown in the water will eventually reach the mainland. God's currents will carry it to its destination. Help will come when needed. Usually, there is suffering before glory or suffering with glory.

Joseph was a child of renewal. He was born late in Jacob's life, just before his father left Laban. Whereas most of his brothers were brought up in Laban's land, Joseph was influenced greatly by the Kidron factor, where his father wrestled with God and prevailed. He lived with a different man than his brothers had – with someone who had been changed. This influenced him greatly. Joseph had seen the effects of renewal. His brothers' war against him was based on their failure to heed the guidance in Psalm 37:1. 'Be not envious...'

Joseph's brothers were envious of his position within the family. Solomon says, 'A sound heart is the life of the flesh: *but envy*, the rottenness of the bones.'[161] They ganged up on him because they envied him, and we envy people but covet things. Luke picks up this same story and theme in the New Testament. 'And the patriarchs, *moved with envy* [emphasis mine], sold Joseph into Egypt: but God was with him.'[162] Envy is the root of almost every sin against the brethren. It prevents peace and causes unrest. The Bible is clear: 'For where you have envy [jealousy] and selfish ambition, there you find disorder and every evil practice.'[163] The psalmist takes the offensive and encourages a positive mind-set in the rest of Psalm: 'Trust in the

Lord,' 'Delight thyself in the Lord,' 'Commit thy way to the Lord,' and finally, 'Rest in the Lord.' The four legs on the stool of life!

Thus, 'Sin may hinder God's plans but it cannot defeat his purposes.'[164] In no case is it possible to bring good out of evil, but good can be brought about in spite of evil. God turned the methodology Joseph's brothers planned to use to destroy him into a good plan for Israel's survival. In Psalm 105:17–19, we read, 'He sent a man before them, even Joseph, who was sold for a servant: Whose feet they hurt with fetters: he was laid in iron: Until the time that his word came: the word of the LORD tried him.'

Basic preparation in life

If we don't have it in prison, we won't have it in the city. And it came to pass; it always does! Joseph was fitted for the throne in the dungeon. Don't blame your circumstances for failure. Use them to mount yourself up to victory. Be positive and rejoice in the prospect of achieving in spite of adversity.[165] 'Wisdom and virtue will shine in the narrowest spheres. A good man will do well wherever he is, and will be a blessing even in bonds and banishment; for the Spirit of the Lord is not bound nor banished, witness St. Paul.'[166] Paul writing to the Pilippians states that his imprisonment served better for the gospel. Accordingly, Joseph was imprisoned for the benefit of Israel when the famines came.[167]

He showed religious principle, not passion. Passion can be born in revivals and can evaporate with the seasons just as quickly as it came. Principles last because they are based on hidden values – values that are independent of externals. Principles come from an inner source unaffected by external issues. He had no borrowed religion; it was his own. He was a man of God who lived by God, in God, and for God. His religion was not pumped up; nor was his devotion mechanical.

Fruitfulness is the outcome of the root, not of labour. Vines do not suddenly decide to work for grapes; it is their nature to bear them. Moses' stick laid before the Lord blossomed and fruited overnight; it was the Lord's presence from which the blossoms sprung. The stick just lay still. This is a lesson we should learn early in our spiritual walk. We cannot achieve fruit, for the making of fruit is the work of the Spirit. You may possess a library catalogue but never read a book. We may have all knowledge of the truth but not act upon any of it. 'He that has a well deep within is beyond the enemy's power.'[168] Moses had a well, not a land spring for surface water can become contaminated with pollutants and taste of earth. People always turn brooks into sewers. Tapes, meetings, and books are watercourses: God is the well.

Minimal epilogue, maximum import

God does not have to say much to reveal a man's character. It is said of Joseph, 'God was with him.'[169] That was sufficient. About Enoch, it is said, 'He walked with God.'[170] Moses was called the meekest man on earth.[171] John the Apostle was 'the disciple whom Jesus loved'.[172] And John the Baptist – there was none greater. 'For I say to you, among those born of women there is not a greater prophet than John the Baptist; but he who is least in the kingdom of God is greater than he.'[173] John recognised Jesus from the womb.

When obituaries are spoken, we tend to suppress the errors of the way and only highlight the good deeds; not so the Bible. It says about David, the sweet psalmist, 'And when He had removed him, He raised up for them David as king, to whom also He gave testimony and said, "I have found David the son of Jesse, a man after My own heart, who will do all My will."'[174] In the matter of Bathsheba, David is named and exposed. But in the life of Joseph, there is nothing to expose.

When God is with a man, He is for a man. When God is for a man, that man will become successful. Almost everyone wants to be successful. Very few realise that they are if God is for them. A sign that we are becoming successful is that the enemies of the Lord become our enemies. If we were not disturbing the realm of darkness, we would not suffer temptation, trial, condemnation, and attack.

The vicissitude of victory

God's presence did not shield Joseph from the woman's seduction. Nor did it relieve the prison regime. He was sold by his brethren, slandered by Potiphar's wife, and forgotten by the butler. On the whole, quite a painful life. But God was with him! 'When troubles elbow their way into our lives we are slow to hear anyone but ourselves. When our plans are interrupted, we erupt. When we are inconvenienced, we are incensed. Then, when anyone tries to tell us anything, we are anything but swift to hear.' However, hear God in it all. His voice will speak through the tumult.

But 'it came to pass' – what does this phrase mean? Well, all things come to pass – eventually. Joseph had a double portion through his sons. Each one became the head of a tribe. 'And now your two sons, Ephraim and Manasseh [two sons amid the twelve tribes], who were born to you in the land of Egypt before I came to you in Egypt, are mine; as Reuben and Simeon, they shall be mine.'[175] God is often preparing our life for our descendants. He will realise His will in those who follow. We are but the beginning of the plan, not the middle and the end. When God is with a person, he or she reigns over circumstances.[176]

Joseph was seventeen when he was in charge of Potiphar's household and thirty when he became ruler of Egypt. He didn't change towards his God or in his duty to man. Wherever he went, he ministered to the needs of others. His life was productive in every circumstance. He managed the Egyptians' affairs, he managed the prison, and eventually he controlled Egypt. He started with his father's command to look after his brethren. He progressed to one man's household and then to the prison with all its inmates and then to the whole of the land of Egypt. If you want to preach to the multitudes, start with a Sunday school class. Be diligent with the young, and God may give you the old. We never know where our diligence will lead us. God fashions all people of faith according to His purpose.

From opposition to opportunity

Joseph was lord of the bread and dispensed it at his will. There were sixty-six people descended from Jacob at this time. His last son Benjamin had ten children. This is a great need. To feed ourselves is dire, but to have so many dependants is crucial. The need of everyone is bread. What is happening around this globe in many countries is happening in many lives through this world. There is a famine.

If the hungry person is in desperate straits, so is the person hungry inside his or her soul. Joseph was not just a pure man (which he was, else God wouldn't have walked with him) and not just a passionate man who strove for excellence, but also a prophetic man, who laid up in store for the future. Jesus does that. Joseph interpreted the dream, made provision for the coming years, and made available the storehouses for the needy. Jesus is the same. Joseph was lord of his master's house, lord of the prison, and lord of the bread. These people had clothes, shoes, water, and housing but not bread. Many people today have all the ingredients for life but not the necessary thing. *You can be naked and have bread, but clothed in royal white fur and die of starvation.*

Chapter 9

Blue Diamonds

Pamela, my second wife, and I went to Stratford upon Avon, a medieval town dating from its official charter in 1196. It is close to the Cotswolds, and when it was the major sheep producing area, Stratford was one of the principal towns for processing, marketing, and distribution of sheep and wool. Its smaller Roman Road connects the larger Fosse Way and Icknield Street. In Chipping Camden, about ten miles south from there, the wool barons built their extensive and expensive homes. After parking the car on the outskirts, I noticed brass plaques about 200-millimetres square built in the footpath. The plaques explained that blue diamonds inscribed on the concrete pathway would serve as markers, pointing visitors to the information centre. Follow the blue motifs, and you would arrive at your destination. So we did and soon found our way to the main thoroughfare or shopping centre. It was relatively early, but the shoppers were many. And with added visitors, we were glad it wasn't summer!

As I stood at the traffic lights, I looked left and saw on a corner of two streets a public house called Encore and dated 1605. From its construction and shape, it looked in good condition, although it was clear that it had had its roof replaced. Most roofs last as long as the nails – about ninety years. The clay tiles also laminate with repeated soaking and freezing. However, for 800 years, this town had withstood the seasons and the wear of humanity and is still vibrant and loved. It is one of the greatest holiday attractions in Britain, and justly so, for it is the birthplace of William Shakespeare, who is reckoned by many as the world's greatest playwright – not my favourite reading as a schoolboy! In 1769, David Garrick was responsible for the first real Shakespearian Theatre as a celebration to mark Shakespeare's birthday, but it was washed almost away in two days by torrential rain.

We had come not to delve into history but to collect Pamela's wedding dress from a shop in Sheep Street. Sheep Street was the residential quarter of the town in the sixteenth century and had been rebuilt after the great fire in 1595, although No. 40 Sheep Street dates from 1480, about 300 years before the birth of the United States of America! No wonder Americans like visiting. But as we walked, it came to me that God is *the information centre* of the universe. And He has left blue paint (Bible texts) along the pathways of life – answers to the questions we pose. Humanity needs direction on how to live. And who better to give it than their creator? The Bible clearly says, 'Remember now thy Creator in the days of thy youth.'[177] And it guides us also to live a good life thereafter. Get to the information centre as soon as you can. Follow the blue diamonds diligently, and you will never get lost.

Blue diamonds do exist but contain impurities (hence their colour). But they're very expensive and rarely seen in shops today. I think God's word is as expensive as that. But it contains no impurities. It is precious beyond words. 'The words of the Lord are pure words: as silver tried in a furnace of earth, purified seven times.'[178] It is so sad that people miss that fact and will read anything and everything except God's word. Sometimes information centres are stumped, but God's word never is; there are words for all seasons and occasions. It is always wise to use the Bible as your jewel box. It is rewarding and rich, with a wealth of wisdom. Here's one jewel that should strike solemnity into our hearts: "But they deliberately forget that long ago by God's word the heavens existed and the earth was formed out of water and by water. By these waters also the world of that time was deluged and destroyed. By the same word the present heavens and earth are reserved for fire, being kept for the Day of Judgment and destruction of ungodly men."[179] Read it slowly and ponder. Let all the facets illumine your inner eye.

Often, we have to admit that we cannot fathom God or follow Him in certainty. And this adds to our trials. For humanity tends to doubt God's intentions towards them. Thus, guidance is often difficult to deduce. But it's not impossible to detect. God is more concerned about our lifestyle direction than we are about knowing His divine will. If we are living according to His will, whatever happens must be by His consent. 'He does according to His will in the army of heaven and among the inhabitants of the earth. No one can restrain His hand or say to Him, "What have You done?"'[180] God can do what he will, when he wills, to whomever he wills, because He is God. Job philosophises thus, 'But He is unique, and who can make Him change? And whatever His soul desires, that He does.'[181] However, guidance is our right as a child of God, bequeathed by the one who has planned and designed all things. Paul said confidently, 'In Him also we have obtained an inheritance, being predestined according to the purpose of Him who works all things according to the counsel of His will.'[182]

God has a definitive plan. We, as his children, are part of that plan. He will bring his purpose into the world, and establish His kingdom through artifices unsought and not thought of by humanity. Jeremiah states unequivocally, 'For I know the thoughts that I think toward you, says the LORD, thoughts of peace and not of evil, to give you a future and a hope.'[183] Guidance is an indispensable necessity as well as a wonderful privilege; it allows for inner harmony and eliminates inner discord. Since each person is unique and distinctive, God can use every aspect of heredity, environment, temperament, and talent to guide an individual, for God's inestimable comprehension strategises with immeasurable compassion and empathy.

On a personal note, looking back on a blessed life, I can say with great conviction that God knows best and can bring about His purposes with consummate ease. In 1973, I was invited to Greenock

Elim Church, together with Reverend Eldin Corsie, to preach at their Easter Convention. I opened the series on Good Friday, and afterwards, on the Saturday, Eldin invited me to London to be his associate minister at Kensington Temple. Having considered all aspects of the new position and the move it would require, I decided not to accept that honour. But my wife prayed that, if that church was to be for me, God would keep the position available to me later. Eleven years later, in 1984, on 25 May, I received a phone call that changed my life forever. It was from Reverend Wynne Lewis, the new senior minister of Kensington Temple. He invited me to be his associate; I accepted.

I was to retire in August of that year at fifty as a senior lecturer and subject tutor for three degrees but didn't welcome London in any respect. And I struggled to accept the invitation. I lived in Solihull in a large bungalow I had just finished remodelling. The bungalow was situated on a third of an acre overlooking a monastery of seventeen acres. It was idyllic. However, Job said, 'That which I feared has come upon me.'[184] My second son was enrolled in Bart's Medical School, and my short and infrequent trips to London through busy Whitechapel had put me off that city forever.

In desperation, I turned to the scriptures. And in my daily reading, I saw this text: 'For the Levites left their common-lands and their possessions and came to Judah and Jerusalem.'[185] Jerusalem was the capital, as was London. I was a priest of God. I had to accept that God had just confirmed His will for my life. At the interview, I had asked why I was wanted in Notting Hill. 'We do not have a teacher,' was the simple reply. My second daily reading was even more definite. It read, 'For a long time Israel has been without...a teaching priest.'[186] I knew God had waylaid me, and my future had been decided.

However, God was not finished, and he gave me a third text several weeks later as I pondered His prospective will. This is what he said: *'And at my table were one hundred and fifty Jews and rulers, besides those who came to us from the nations around us.'*[187] Little did I know or realise that, within nine months of arriving at Kensington Temple, I would be elected superintendent of London with fifty-five churches (150 leaders) and many nations represented from a multi-ethnic culture. I have found God's word to be infallible.

Arriving in London, my wife and I bought a house in North Wembley. We lived there for twenty years. But there came a time when we needed to downsize. My wife kept jogging my memory about moving, and I kept forgetting! However, one day she was particularly insistent. So I went to my study to read God's word on the matter. My daily reading contained this text: 'We moved along the coast with difficulty and came to a place called 'Fair Havens, near the town of Lasea.'[188] My house was called Fair Havens. My deduction was that we had arrived, so there was no need to move.

As I put my Bible back on the shelf, God said quite distinctly, *Read it in another translation.* So I pulled out the one next to it (I had thirty different Bibles on that particular shelf). It read thus: 'And docked at Good Harbour [Fair Havens]. But it was *not the best harbour* for staying the winter.' God's word was clear. My wife and I were in the winter of our lives and ought to move; his guidance was simple, clear, and direct.

So we moved. That is my kind of guidance. We may not want to go where He leads or be involved with situations akin to that leading. But in the end, He will bring all things to pass. His plans are far-reaching, and He rarely reveals all His moves at once.

In my early twenties, when I was pioneering my first church, I was leading the evening service in the school that we'd rented while our church was under construction. The site was almost opposite the school, so as we assembled, we could see the progress and waited impatiently while we finished the church. It was self-built to save money and a real pioneering project. That Sunday night, my elder brother entered the service late and purposefully walked up to me. He whispered, 'It's gone – the church; the wind's hit it.'

At first, I thought he was joking. And then I remembered hearing the rising sound of the wind as I had entered the school. I was training as a civil engineer and realised the full implications. We stopped the service and raced across the road. There it almost was – a shattered heap, a timber-framed building with a brick front. The front remained but not much else.

Outwardly I was strong, resolute, and determined. It was a brave face for the crowd; inwardly, I was crying. I had been through a tough schedule. Enrolled at a local university, I spent three nights a week taking an external degree and spent an additional two nights on assignments and study. All day on Saturdays, I physically built the church. On Saturday nights, I prepared for the Sunday morning sermon; Sunday afternoons were prep time for the Sunday night service. All that work, and now it lay in tatters. I simply said, 'See you on Saturday, men.' I don't think I could have said anything else. And with that, I went home.

The next Saturday, I was ready to start again. I began clearing away the debris and sorting out what could be saved and used. To my surprise, a large group of people from the church arrived. Some Saturdays, I had been there by myself. And sometimes it had been just my wife and me. But now we were inundated. I watched with not only pleasure and excitement but with a growing sense that God was in this.

Before the disaster, the people had responded sporadically to the project of building our church, while I had been the mainstay and the leader it was out in front of the project. Now I was swamped with eager hands. The demolition had gelled the church. Prior to that incident, the members of the congregation were almost strangers to each other – people in some kind of loose relationship. Now they were galvanised into team action. Soon, the building arose from the splinters, and the patched, Pentecostal, prayer and praise centre emerged. Neighbours who witnessed the catastrophe and who regularly passed by came to see what kind of people would be motivated to rebuild it – they stayed and were saved. This was God's sovereign will, of course!

The supposed disaster had been the birth of the church. Prior to the 'catastrophe', I had thought we were a church. But really, we had just been an assembled crowd. The adversity had drawn the people together; I saw my dream become their dream. Peace returned. God was in the shadows and the sound of the wind: *Think of the benefits, son!*

Something good can come from apparent calamity. God's plans are never thwarted. The Cross was not a defeat but a victory. If we praise God in adversity, we'll find we have peace in perplexity and provision in necessity. Turning negatives into positives is a spiritual art that should be practised every day. There are always opportunities to turn apparent disasters into a springboard for victory.

We fight, kick, and scream at the inevitable, and God wins in the end. God makes an announcement through the varying vicissitudes of life, and yet we struggle to alter His will, knowing inwardly that it is the only place where we will find real peace. Naaman viewed Jordan as I viewed London. Yet it was those seven dirty dips that healed him. Peace comes when we hear God. But we don't want to hear him because he often changes our plans, plans that are manufactured with self-interest paramount.

Jesus said to Peter, "'I must go to Jerusalem, and suffer many things from the elders and chief priests and scribes, and be killed, and be raised the third day.' Then Peter took Him aside and began to rebuke Him, saying, 'Far be it from You, Lord; this shall not happen to You!'"[189] [This is a modern day part translation from the Century Bible]. If Jesus died, Peter would have no destiny. Or so he thought. He believed that Jesus had to live in order for him to fulfil his personal plans. Unconsciously, we manipulate God, or think we can, to ensure our future. On the mount, Moses and Elijah, two Old Testament witnesses, spoke to Jesus 'concerning his death' – that was God's will. It often is.

The words of Jesus to Peter ring true through all avenues of life: 'You are not mindful of the things of God, but the things of men.' We are bombarded by the world's idea of spirituality; through the media, our perceptions are guided and moulded by their opinion. Sensing Jesus in the midst of life is not an easy task, especially if we listen too much to other voices. It is no wonder that peace is a rare quality in today's busy church scene. The whole thrust of modern preaching is to make champions, but too many of these so-called heroes are rusting away inside.

The liner *Queen Mary* was sold by the British to the county of Long Beach, Los Angeles, where it was to be converted to a museum, hotel, and restaurant. When it arrived in America, the ship's new owners decided to refurbish the ship and, in consequence, unbolted the funnels and lifted them to the quayside. As they touched the tarmacadam, they disintegrated into hundreds of pieces. Upon analysis, the owners discovered that there were twenty coats of paint and no funnels – the funnels had rusted away from the inside!

David said, 'Fret not thyself.'[190] The word *fret* means 'to rust or worry'. Worry is internal decay, encapsulated by Milton's words, 'Care sat on his faded cheek.' It gnaws away at our serenity and confidence and leaves us hopefully, but not expectantly, dispelling the shadows of our apparitions in the night-time of experience. However, those of us who are Christ's, have an assurance that He is our intercessor[191] and prays for us daily. And who knows, although we cannot tell him to do so, He may send an angel for our safety. He also says, 'Casting all your care upon him; for He cares for you.'[192] And scripture tells us, 'Don't worry about anything; instead, pray about everything.'[193]

Not the end of the line

God's call on our lives will lead us into avenues of ministry and service that will both reveal Him and change us. *But the problem is that we often think the track is the terminus.* We reach a certain point and think we've arrived. The guidance seems to stop, so we presume that's where we're going to stay. What appears to be the buffers is still a long way from our destination.

Two people walk along a beach. They both pick up a shell. One of them looks at it and quickly tosses it into the sea. The other holds onto what they have found and tries to visualise the creature that lived inside it and how the oceans came to have such life in the first place. To the first person, a shell means finality, the end. But to the other, it leads to much more. Someone takes a walk along a clifftop on a wild winter's night. The weather turns even worse, so seeing nothing but the gathering storm and concerned for his or her safety and comfort, the person races for shelter. Another person taking the same path marvels at the howling wind and the crashing waves on the jagged rocks below. He or she thrills to the power of the sea and its melodies, its hissing and groaning. A symphony is composed and written.

So many Christians are so caught up with their present experiences and situations, especially when they are in difficulty, that they fail to see positive things beyond them. They think they have reached the end of the road, but God only means it to be a pit stop on the way to victory. History tends to be taught as a succession of strong men pillaging, raping, and plundering lands, of building empires through unquenched greed. To some people, it is a tale of a crimson stream of anger and dominion. But there are others who can trace the finger of God through the violent rise and fall of nations. In the shattered dreams of myriad civilisations, there is the cry of human hearts searching for truth and God's ultimate answer in Jesus. Beyond the many crowns, the monarch of time and eternity reigns over all the earth. Empires fail, fall, and are swept away like dust. Yet those who have eyes to see can acclaim a kingdom that cannot be shaken.

To the rescue

The first two verses of the Bible say, 'In the beginning God created the heavens and the earth. Now the earth was formless and empty, darkness was over the deep and the Spirit of God was hovering over the waters.'[194] It's not just a statement about creation and the beginning of time. It's about humanity in its helpless state before God and a picture of His divine intervention. Human beings are fallen creatures because of sin, and there is darkness and desolation in their soul.

Humanity is without spiritual form and empty. They have no divine life in themselves. God could have left them helpless with the mists of gloom rolling over their soul. Instead, He sent His Spirit to hover and bring new life out of the darkness. God came to the rescue of a world in turmoil. Out of His matchless creative spirit of love, He made something from nothing. In this wondrous act, God brought His energy to bear, taking the wreckage of humanity swirling around in darkness blacker than black and bringing meaning out of chaos and order out of confusion.

For people who hand their lives over to Christ, the quickening Spirit of God brings direction, light, and fruitfulness into their lives. The beginning of Genesis doesn't just describe God's creation of planet Earth; it lays out the way to the restoration of man's fallen soul.[195] God can do extraordinary things with individuals. He came to a rich old Assyrian and persuaded him to sell his belongings and swop comfort for the hardships of travel in the wilderness. He responded in faith, and 'not knowing whither' (to use the title of Oswald Chambers' book on Genesis) got as far as Haran. That seemed to be about it as far as God's guidance was concerned. So father Terah, son Abraham, and family set up home, started a new business, found pastures for the flocks, and settled down to a comfortable routine again.

That's typical of God's dealings. Just when we think we're settled for the years ahead, if not for the rest of our lives, He comes to us and tells us to get going again. Haran was only a staging post for Abraham. As soon as he had buried his father, God moved him on.[196] Haran was many miles from triumph's terminus. There were still lots more hills to climb and valleys to go through.

Often we obey God and, in faith, move out into a new field of service, thinking it is His final will for us when, in reality, we have hardly begun to walk. We are concentrating so much on living that we forget the route. Because we are so taken with the decision to follow the master, we mistake where we are. We think we have travelled far but, like Peter, have only just stepped on to the water.[197] We must not restrict God from leading us beyond our limited horizons.

Transit station

If ever there was a man who thought he had reached the end of his journey, it was Moses. Brought up by royalty and skilled in leadership and the arts of the war, Moses was destined for the Egyptian throne – until he became incensed about gross human rights violations against his own people, the enslaved Israelites. He was so angry that he took matters into his hands, killing a soldier and then fleeing for his life from Pharaoh's wrath.

He exchanged the palace for the monotony of the desert. His sandaled feet moving from grazing ground to grazing ground, his face blasted by the wind-borne sand until he looked like the scrub he traversed, he oversaw sheep for forty long years. That's the length of time most modern men work for their pensions. As time went by, so too went Moses' ambition to see the deliverance of his people. He grew content with each day's labour in this barren yet peaceful place, with sleep after darkness had fallen. And he wanted that peace to continue undisturbed.

God had other ideas. Moses was a long way from the terminus of his destiny. In fact, the most exciting journey of his life lay ahead. The desert was a transit station and a training ground. Forty years remained for him to be a vital instrument in God's plans to shape the nation of Israel. Moses' next stop was the palace to confront Pharaoh. God would use him to break Egypt's grip on His people, lead them out of captivity, and take them almost into the Promised Land.

We have a tendency when stuck in one place for a long time to lose sight of goals and let dreams die. To some of us, this is welcome, and we are lulled into thinking that God is content as we are. Then we are surprised when we find we have arrived not at the end of our journey but, rather, at the end of its beginning. We mistook the red lights for a 'road closed' sign.

A young man enjoyed being his father's favourite son. He had an eye-catching coat to prove it. He had dreams of grandeur, and unfortunately, he boasted about the revelations he had been given. To his brothers, he was pompous and overbearing. So they decided to get him to take a long journey – into slavery. That, as far as they were concerned, was the terminus for boastful brother Joseph. Father Jacob thought so too when he was shown the precious coat, now bloody. He mourned over the assumed death of his beloved son. Terminus was written on his heart.[198]

Prison to palace

Joseph, too, must have thought he had reached the terminus of life. Enticed and then falsely accused of rape by Pharaoh's promiscuous wife and incarcerated in prison, rejected and forgotten, he must have questioned whether those dreams of rulership had come from God after all. But it was there, in that dark place, that God stepped in. In one day, Joseph went from the foul, rat-infested hole to the throne room of Egypt, dressed in a ruler's robe.[199] What Joseph thought was a terminus was actually a thoroughfare.

There was a greedy young man destined for greatness who played a dirty trick on his elder brother. Having gained what he wanted, he left home in a hurry to escape the inevitable wrath. On the way to Uncle Laban's ranch that night, the trickster slept fitfully. He knew he had done wrong. God had promised him the blessing, but he couldn't wait. He had gained it by his subterfuge and craftiness, aided and abetted by his scheming mother.[200] Now his life was in danger. It seemed that he, too, had reached a terminus. (Twenty years later, he still thought that, as Genesis 32:6–8 reveals). Yet God met with Jacob on that dark, dark night, giving him a vision for the future and assuring him that, despite what he had, done the divine presence would go with him.[201] He woke up realising that Bethel was not the end but 'the gate of heaven'. Our rock pillows can be the start of new adventures with God.

An allegory – An open door: An application

Patricia and I were strolling down Twickenham High Street enjoying the clear blue sky, cold sunshine, and abnormal winter weather.

Turning into our favourite Italian restaurant, we had our tea and croissants ready for the longer walk down by the river. Patricia decided to go the restroom, so I ventured outside and sat at a table in the thin sunshine and waited. I watched the world go hurrying by and suddenly realised that fifteen minutes or more had passed, long enough for any normal function or malfunction! I went inside and approached the rear of the café, near where the toilets were situated, only to find the owner and his assistant frantically trying to open the door to the women's toilet. The latch had malfunctioned, and Patricia was trapped inside, and had been for nearly twenty minutes.

I leaned on the opening archway to the toilets and watched as they tried to open the door and, within a few moments after their having tried for a long time, gained access. Patricia exited smiling and saying, 'I told you to fetch my husband. He is a builder and can advise on these things.'

They grimaced in embarrassment, and I just stood, conveying hidden knowledge that would have solved their problem and so avoided their panic.

Off we went for a further walk and eventually returned home. The situation was forgotten, all was well, and we had our exercise. Within a few minutes of arriving home, as I came out of my study into the hall, I heard Patricia hammering on the bathroom door. She was trapped, the lock had failed – a repeat situation. It seemed almost impossible that two such similar occurrences could happen within ninety minutes.

Two things could have gone wrong. The spring mechanism could have failed, or the spindle between the two handles had been cut too short and the slamming of the door over a period had shifted it so that one handle (her side) had failed to catch. I went back into my study and fetched my toolbox, and three minutes later she was set free. In her words, 'The master builder was on the job!' My chest swelled in pride as I put my tools away; practical experience is worth a tonne of theory. Was God trying to teach us something? Well, I'm not sure, but you can always learn something from everyday life.

As Patricia pointed out, because I was a master builder (I have three qualifications in the subject – two degrees and membership of the Chartered [Royal] Insitute of Building) I was able to set her free. And because God is *the* master builder, he can set us free. No door can be closed that he cannot open, and no door he shuts can be opened.[202] His divine toolbox is always ready! The scriptures are replete with situations where He opened doors and set people free.

Paul the Apostle was trapped in an environment of education and bias. He was set free from Phariseeism when God opened his eyes to see the risen Lord and, in effect, opened a door of faith to the Gentiles.[203] Paul could say, 'For a great and effective door has opened to me.'[204] He said the opener of the door was a wise 'master builder',[205] and His master was Jesus Christ, who excelled in everything and was *the* master builder. His words ring true today: 'Behold, I stand at the door, and knock: if any man hear my voice, and open the door, I will come in to him, and will sup with him, and he with me.'[206] The lock is on the inside. Only we can open it. Christ will not force the lock, although he could (he has the technology)! Will you open today? If so, he will come in and fellowship with you in all His love and grace. He will not force the lock.

An allegory – Safe landing

During the second world war, there was a man who invented a parachute that was 100 per cent trustworthy; it didn't matter how big or small the person was who used it, it opened every time and got its user safely to the ground. The key was in the way it was folded. Every part of the parachute had to be carefully and painstakingly placed in certain positions, following the instructions given by the manufacturer. True, achieving the correct folding was sometimes arduous, but the time was well worth the effort when it had the effect of preserving the precious life of every human being who trusted the parachute.

Sometime after the war began, a group of young men known as 'fast folders' entered the packing room. These men so influenced the workers with their new fast and easy method of folding, they completely ignored the instruction book given by the manufacturer. Production increased, and everyone rejoiced that so much time and effort had been saved. The result was that nine out of every ten people who used the parachutes died. When the folders heard about this, they immediately reverted to the maker's instructions – although some resisted, even knowing it was certain death for the parachutist.

They argued that 'fast folding' justified the method despite the fact that safety was compromised – and impatience leads or can lead to death of vision. There are those who think they can circumvent God's will and arrive more quickly at their destiny, taking impetuous action to succeed. God only opens doors (folds the parachute) in His time. He painstakingly wraps the parcel over many years. But when He's done and the parcel is ready, He delivers it by first-class post!

Thus, He arranges things that are remarkable. My first wife was in the Sunday evening service and went from praise to worship and then into *the Presence*. [A whole chapter could be given over to explaining this, but there are times when one comes into the the tangible presence of God that is unmistakable and inexplicable but certainly real]. When you get there, you can ask what you will, and God will answer. Our dog had died, and she was particularly upset. She said to God simply, 'I'm not saying I need a dog, but if you think it's good for me, you'll have to do it, for we do not have the money to buy one.' The service ended, and we went home and prepared supper. We had taken it into the lounge to watch *Antiques Roadshow*, and as we sat eating, the phone rang. At that time of night, calls were usually for her, and as she talked, I realised this call was no exception. She suddenly put her head through the serving hatch and said, 'We have another dog.' She didn't ask if we wanted a dog or if we should have one; she simply announced that we had one. It was clear the deal was done! Someone who was ignorant of her prayer (as was I at the time) had rung to give her £300 for another dog.

We looked for breeding kennels and found two in the Cotswolds. So off we went to explore what was available. But neither presented possibilities for a suitable pet. We stayed overnight in a bed and breakfast in Broadway, and next morning, after breakfast, causally walked up the main street before we left for home. As we strolled along, a man with a black miniature schnauzer, the kind of dog we were looking for, approached us. After talking to him, we learned he had bought his schnauzer from a kennel near London where we lived. We made no delay in visiting it on the way home and bought one of the pups. The mother had been an American champion, and her owner had put an embargo on any of her offspring being shown and had, therefore, reduced the price from £450 to £300. Do you think God was ignorant of that when he caused someone to offer that sum to Patricia? He is sovereign in small and large things and events. It was no accident that the three wise men brought gifts that Joseph and Mary could sell for their upkeep as they migrated to an embalming country – gold, frankincense, and myrrh. God planned well. He always does.

Chapter 10

Fully Fitted Kitchens

*And therefore will the L*ORD *wait, that he may be gracious unto you,*
and therefore will he be exalted...blessed are all they that wait for him.
—Isaiah 30:18

In his steps[207]

'The Israel National Parks Authority has approved a 262 foot-long transparent bridge to be built just below the surface of the Sea of Galilee so visitors can follow in the footsteps of Christ.... After it opens, the contractor, Ron Major, expects up to 800,000 people a year to pay a minimal fee to walk on water. And, yes, lifeguards will be on hand in case anyone strays from the true path.'[208]

If anyone has been to Israel, and I have, he or she knows there is a unique sense of destiny about the country. And guides are quick to point to the places where Jesus ministered. Beverley Shea, Billy Graham's lead singer, who died at 104, used to sing that lovely old hymn, 'I Walked Today Where Jesus Walked,' which he ministered in such a way that was full of pathos and heart-wrenching history. It is, therefore, only natural that technology would one day want to simulate Peter's walking on water.

No doubt, photographs, taken by friends and family will grace mantelpieces across the world, depicting people walking on the

Galilean lake. But perhaps we should rephrase that old hymn and, rather than crooning, 'I walked today where Jesus walked', sing, 'I walked today *as* Jesus walked'. There is a big difference. Humanity cannot produce miracles, but people will do all they can to copy them. The famous football manager 'Cloughie' wrote his autobiography *Walking on Water*. The title came from his ability to do the impossible in human terms. Those who triumph over adversity and trials are often said to be able to walk on water.

Many folk pretend to walk where Jesus walked, but not many can say truthfully, 'I walk *as* Jesus walked.' Walk in grace, walk in truth, walk in holiness, walk in humility, and walk in the Father's will – day after day, year after year; that is a real miracle. The theme woven throughout the New Testament is walking in God. 'In him we live, and move and have our being.'[209]

The only glass bridge under our feet between us and the swirling waters of life is the ultimate sacrifice of Calvary. *No one can see our invisible means of support*, but people can see that we are walking on water. They know that something is supporting us because of how we react in adversity. And we do have a lifeguard – it's the Holy Spirit. He's there in case we slip. Therefore, we have double security.

All those who put their trust in Christ live a miraculous life – daily. The bridge in Galilee is only seventy-nine metres long, but our bridge will reach from time into eternity and beyond, no doubt the longest bridge ever built! You won't suddenly fall off the end, for there is no end. What God does He does well. But it is a toll bridge. To walk along it effectively, we have to deny sight and live by faith – that's the biggest price any of us can pay.

We need to build a bridge while we walk on it. From a biblical viewpoint, as we walk in faith daily, we are successfully building the support system for our life one step at a time. In the film *The Last Crusade*, where Indiana Jones finds the Holy Grail, his final walk is to step off a stone ledge over a valley of sheer stone walls into fresh air, which he does. And as he does, a miraculous bridge appears. His faith was rewarded, and the chalice was found. We are not trying to find the Holy Grail. There is no such thing. But we are endeavouring to reach the destiny designed by God. And inevitably that will mean us walking on water or stepping off the path into fresh air. This is the challenge of the life of faith.

The uncomfortable thing about our walk in life is that humans always want more, and the current generation is no exception. What Harrison Ford's character wanted was the Holy Grail. But no matter how much people earn, they always want more. Experts have found that, irrespective of what people gross, they always estimate that the amount they need to live on is just a bit beyond their means. Many blame it on inflation, which is the loss in purchasing power of a currency unit, such as the pound or dollar, usually expressed as a general rise in the prices of goods and services. However, not only do they want more, they want whatever they want now, not at some future time. This urgency has crept into the church and the lives of some Christians, and they begin to worry God for not providing for them troubled free lives. God seems to say no too often or to delay His answer.

Some Americans have conducted a survey in which people were shown a list of items and asked to first name which ones were essential or crucial for living a good life and then disclose which of those items they owned. They surveyed the same people years later and found that, although many had now acquired most of those items they'd said were crucial but did not own, their list had grown, and they now regarded others things on the list as vital. One illustration was the size of the houses they bought. In the early 1970s, the average new home was 140 square meters (1,484 square feet). But in 2005, this figure had grown to 225 square meters (2,385 square feet) – a 62 per cent increase.

In addition, expectations of what facilities and fittings should come with a house have risen. My first house, purchased in 1959, had one communal first-floor bathroom and no downstairs toilet; today, people would expect ground-floor facilities and a bathroom en suite to the master bedroom in addition to the main bathroom. Back in 1959, the kitchen would have a sink unit, a small coal-burning stove, and a pantry. Now, kitchens are fully fitted, preferably with a granite top; extractor fan; a fridge, freezer, and dishwasher; and, of course, central heating.

The interesting fact that emerged was that, no matter what people bought two decades ago, the disposable income that was left over after taxes and paying bills was approximately 10 per cent, and now it is zero. This depletion could be attributed to the pressure to spend more and live at a new income level. It is thought that the new trend is not the old scenario of 'keeping up with the Joneses' but, rather, as Robert H. Frank would say, the 'cascading wealth effect'. It seems that those at the top of the income distribution who enjoy more luxuries increase the standard of living for those people below them. This means that coffee makers and toasters now come in stainless steel.

No matter how much effort the government puts into controlling inflation, in the end, we, *the people*, need to control our expectations. The solution cannot be simple, but being a Christian can help. We are not, or should not be, influenced by possessions; at death, we lose everything except those internal qualities of the soul. Perhaps our yearning should not be for a two-car garage but for a terrace house up there in heaven. What we sow in the lifestyle we lead now we reap in that heavenly future. But *we have lost the fact of eternity*!

As social conditions in the West improve, the need to dwell on themes of eternity has diminished. The church no longer sings, 'Jerusalem the golden, with milk and honey blest'. Its yearning for golden streets, silver lakes, and gates of pearl has been replaced with a triumphalism that makes earth into heaven. The serene sunlight of that celestial city is shunned for the infrared lamp of an eternal holiday. The land where roses never fade has been replaced with tinted silk blooms, which only need dusting.

No longer do preachers exhort weary pilgrims plodding to the place of bliss, for the land of pure delight has already begun. Our mega-churches suggest they are the satellites of heaven itself, and the combination of hype and holiness answers the need for the upward flight to an everlasting spring. Name it and claim it seems to be the answer. You can be rich here, and when you are rich, you don't need God, except in ill health. It's a pleasant mode of Christianity!

The mood has changed since the turn of the century. Whereas the gospel express to happy land was the secondary focus, it is now the prime point of concern, and the journey occupies our attention. Nearly everybody wants a first-class seat. Forgotten is that 'treasure in heaven that will not be exhausted, where no thief comes near and no moth destroys. For where your treasure is, there your heart will be also.'[210] The problem is identified and intensified by a lack of teaching on the second coming of Christ. It is now a distant dream that might happen!

The lost art

The history of humanity in scripture is that they have to learn to wait for and to wait on God. Patience should predominate in the Christian lifestyle. Very rarely do we read of God waiting for us. But, in a sense, the two ideas are synonymous, for man waiting for God to act is God waiting to be gracious. So they complement each other. God gave a promise to Adam about the seed and the serpent,[211] and humanity had to wait for the dawning of Immanuel. In another sense, God had to await for his predetermined counsel to be fulfilled: 'Him, being delivered by the determinate counsel and foreknowledge of God, ye have taken, and by wicked hands have crucified and slain.'[212]

Anger and disbelief often registers in the hearts of those who have experienced God's delays. Their frustration is evident, and there are very few words to pacify the demands they make. 'Hope deferred makes the heart sick: but when the desire cometh, it is a tree of life.'[213] The bland and not too confident grunts of encouragement such people give, in an attempt to support their crumbling faith, are little more than squeaks of irritation. David the psalmist found himself in the midst of such a time of trouble (Psalm 73) and wondered why God seemed to bless the ungodly. Meanwhile he and his people were unrewarded by apparent divine inaction. It seemed that God was waiting. Or was it wanting? 'Rest in the LORD, and wait patiently for him: fret not thyself because of him who prospers in his way, because of the man who brings wicked devices to pass.'[214] And in a later verse, 'For evildoers shall be cut off: but those that wait upon the LORD, they shall inherit the earth.'[215] Those who wait will eventually see God act. But why does He wait so long and so often? Let's suggest some reasons why He waits. As we do this, we will discover several immutable ideas, not too far along the road of discovery.

God's delays are not denials

The life of Abram tells us this quite clearly. The call and promise of God in his life were definite and rewarding. However, he had to wait at least twenty-five years for the promise to reach fulfilment. He went out of Ur when he was seventy-five and had Isaac when he was almost a hundred. 'Now the LORD had said unto Abram, Get thee out of thy country, and from thy kindred, and from thy father's house, unto a land that I will shew thee.'[216] The Lord had also said, 'And I will bless them that bless thee, and curse him that curses thee: and in thee shall all families of the earth be blessed.'[217] This promise could only be fulfilled through the promised son, and God didn't exactly deny (rush to fulfil it)!

God's no is often only a temporary hiccup in our programme. But because we don't have foreknowledge of events and circumstances, we find that trusting may be difficult. When God said get out of *that* land and into *this* land, Abram didn't know what it meant; all he had to hold onto was the promise. At Ur's checkout gate, he was handed a plastic carrier bag, or so it must have seemed to him. It must have looked frail, but in his ignorance and blind faith, he believed God, and it was counted as payment. Years later, God acted. But first he had to prove he *was* God so that the onlookers of history would know that this was a divine deed, which would reinforce His immutability. 'Therefore sprang there even of one, and him as good as dead [or, as one translation puts it, 'shrivelled'], so many as the stars of the sky in multitude, and as the sand which is by the sea shore innumerable.'[218]

God's delay is not desertion

The psalm of Jesus, which prophesises his death, reads, 'My God, my God, why have you forsaken me? Why are you so far from helping me, and from the words of my roaring?'[219] This seems to suggest God's delay in rescuing His Son, which could well fill us with apprehension. If Jesus is not safe, then who is? Jesus was experiencing separation for the first time. His constant exclamation in the New Testament was that He and the Father were one: 'Holy Father, keep through thine own name those whom you have given me that they may be one, as we are.'[220]

Siamese twins experience high trauma when they are separated, but Jesus was not only joined at the head, hip, and heel; He was one with God. God was waiting, doing nothing, as His Son suffered. You may think this was cruel, a real desertion. But the divine plan demanded courage. Jesus said, 'The Son of man came not to be ministered unto, but to minister, and to give his life a ransom for many.'[221] And scripture also says, 'For God so loved the world that he gave his only begotten Son, that whosoever believeth in him should not perish, but have everlasting life.'[222] There could be no greater love than this, and no greater desertion in the short time. He waited to be gracious, and graciousness has about it an understanding of 'accommodating', of wanting to help in any way possible. If it is possible to understand, God also suffered pain in the separation, but the great eternal plan of redemption was actioned.

God's delays are for development

History reveals that God puts His people when and where he wants to fulfil the destiny of His great purposes. Joseph was such a man for such a time. 'He sent a man before them, even Joseph, who was sold for a servant. Whose feet they hurt with fetters: he was laid in iron.'[223] All he had done was to speak out his dream. 'And Joseph dreamed a dream, and he told it his brethren: and they hated him yet the more.'[224] There are some things we need to keep quiet about because others don't have the grace to receive them.

But, and here we pause, for God's *but* is better than any scheme or malicious act of man. God knew that, thirteen years later, Jacob and his sons would need food, and he set in motion a plan. And as scripture tells us, 'Surely the wrath of man shall praise thee.'[225] He turns on its head the anger and injury of men, and makes it praise His great name.

Changing the interpretive slant, we find that, in this saga of reinstatement, God was preparing his vessel to become a great man. The route was mapped out, and the plan was secure. Everything that happened was part of the great purpose. God was maturing the man, and the delay was part of the development. We never know what God ultimately wants us to be. Abram was seventy-five, Moses was eighty, and Jesus thirty before each commenced his life's work. The miracle is that Jesus could have started at twelve!

God's delays are for healing

'Then said Jesus unto them plainly, "Lazarus is dead."'[226] When Lazarus was ailing and growing ever sicker, Jesus waited. If Jesus had gone when Lazarus was sick, the healing might have been disparaged, but now that the man reeked (John 11:29) it had to be a miracle. Only God can raise the dead and create life. God's delays ultimately bring a greater miracle to the fore; He never underestimates the effect of the divine presence. There is more glory in raising the dead than in curing a headache. We may be unwittingly part of a process that will bring great glory to God, and in that delay will come the enlargement of His great name. We should not trouble God with our petty impatience.

In this instance, only after the angel of death had visited, could Jesus come. For he was to reveal to the people of Bethany the real godlike nature that was his. This was authentic love. To have hastened would have been to have denied the people revelation, which could only be manifest through the miracle. Jesus was to prove to them that the resurrection was not only to be in the end of time, but that *he was the resurrection*. It was his permanent nature. In him was life.

We often find out more about God when He delays than when He rushes to our aid. The distant days of resurrection give meagre hope for the immediate need. Unless God had delayed His appearance at the Red Sea, Egypt's forces would not have been destroyed. We need a present God of resurrection, who can deal with life-and-death issues now. His delay at the graveside was to put in the grave the doubt that He cannot work against the odds. 'Jesus said unto her, "I am the resurrection, and the life: he that believeth in me, though he was dead, yet shall he live."'[227] There is a difference between *faith in resurrection* and *resurrection faith*.

God's delays are for His glory

God's one great desire is that He is glorified in all His ways. His great love at Calvary is an act of glory. His forgiveness is the same. The raising of Lazarus was similarly blessed. When it is outside human ingenuity to make something happen then it has to be God who does so. The author of Psalms has it this way: 'Wait on the LORD: be of good courage, and he shall strengthen thine heart: wait, I say, on the LORD.'[228] There comes a time in our experience where we must rely on God, or nothing can ever be achieved. 'My soul, wait thou only upon God; for my expectation is from him.'[229] Our problem is that our hopes often get sidetracked, and we expect others to help, when in reality, for His glory, it has to be only God. 'Wait on the LORD, and keep his way, and he shall exalt thee to inherit the land: when the wicked are cut off, you shalt see it.'[230] If we trace God's glory through the scriptures, we will see that He responds in the fullness of time or at the right moment. Each time, His glory is manifest.

God's delays might be due to our sin

'And therefore will the LORD wait, that he may be gracious unto you, and therefore will he be exalted, that he may have mercy upon you.'[231]

In our text, God is waiting to show how much mercy and grace He really has. His chosen people have wandered off and made Egypt their ally, trusting in the strength of a foreign power. The bows and chariots of others are to be their salvation, but salvation belongs only to our God. Life is a question of whether we will walk with God at all times; in all situations, good or bad; and in all trials of faith. The flesh has a tendency to veer towards earthly temptations; "that you *put off*, concerning your former conduct, the old man which grows corrupt according to the deceitful lusts, and be renewed in the spirit of your mind, and that you put on the new man which was created according to God, in true righteousness and holiness."[232] We, therefore, substitute our answers because of God's delays.

Jesus, after the resurrection, said to His eleven disciples, 'Meet me in Galilee.' And he was not there when they arrived. He delayed, and there was no apparent reason for his lateness. He was not late with His birth or his death. Why delay now? Perhaps He was testing the initiative of the disciples; while He was among them, they had food, shelter, transport, and direction. Their greatest priority here by the lake was food, so they did what they could – they went fishing. The old regime had died with Jesus; they were now alone, and back to work they went. Nothing wrong with that – better that than slouch and groan and blame God; at least eating a few fish would lift their mood a little.

However, Jesus did come after they had toiled and caught nothing. But on his instruction, they tried a left-handed throw (right hand side of the ship) and caught so many fish the ship began to sink. So by doing the ridiculous, they achieved the impossible. That is the lesson of life. Here was Jesus still teaching them that, when He is around and His words are obeyed, we can be remarkable. We can, in effect, achieve the unachievable. With each divine delay, there is a possibility of a new parable of wonder. Do not despise delays.

Chapter 11

The Love Bug

A few years ago, a truant Filipino schoolboy caused widespread disruption to computer systems around the world. He created an email virus known as ILOVEYOU. The virus infected Parliament, Barclays, BT, the BBC, and News International, paralysing their systems before moving on. ILOVEYOU, which attacked computers via the Microsoft Outlook System, originated in Manila. It hit Hong Kong and then spread swiftly across time zones to Europe.

In Denmark, Parliament, ministries, and major television companies were affected. The Swiss government and several banks shut their computer systems down as the virus attacked, and 500,000 systems were hit in Spain. In America, Congress had to shut down its email systems after several Congressmen fell for the virus. One leading antivirus manufacturer said the virus has cost British companies millions of pounds because they had been switching off their email systems, and to do so was effectively to turn their cash flow off.

The snare of this virus was that it arrived on your computer screen, apparently from someone you know, with an invitation to open the enclosed love letter. In that act of opening the virus, it adds itself to the Windows directory and register and remains whether the computer is shut down or not. It then invades the email directory and sends itself to all the addresses it finds. It continues by working through the computer, deleting files and, thus, paralysing the system.

Experts were able to eliminate the virus after several hours, but by that time, millions of pounds worth of damage had been done. The designer of this virus chose the right subject; it was a masterly piece of infiltration. After food, humanity wants love. The need to eat and the need to give and receive love dominate society. They have since humankind was created. Eve took the fruit in the Garden of Eden, and Adam, because he loved her, took it also – there it is in Genesis chapter 3.

One of HICC's leadership asked me if I had received the virus on my computer because they had at their workplace. I said, 'No, I wouldn't open anything that said, "I love you", knowing that it would be a hoax. Perhaps if it had said, "I hate you", I might have done!'

Anyhow, a married man shouldn't open such invitations unless they come from his wife. It was this secret desire within many people to be admired and loved illicitly by someone other than their spouses (providing they were married) that caused much of the problem. I can well understand single people opening an email with promises of love; seeking love is a prime component of their lives and expectations. But married people should have been more cautious.

It's amazing how such a simple statement can expose hidden desire, and I have found over many years that much of my revelatory gifting is contained in letter writing. I often send letters to people, and the most innocuous statement can cause profound ripples, as I unconsciously touch something in that person's spirit. It's called a Word of Knowledge, one of the twenty-five gifts of the Holy Spirit.

God has sent an email with an attachment to all humanity, and it is called 'I love *you*'. This message is found in the Bible time and again. When downloaded into your soul, you'll find it will infect you forever. There is no cure. But this message brings health to the system, not damage. Once it is opened, it will attach itself to the Windows directory of your soul and start deleting corrupt files, replacing them with a virus-free programme. For the first time, the computer of your life will start working properly because God's 'virus' will mend and heal and not destroy – divine love fulfils us to the absolute. If you get an Internet message from God saying, 'I love *you*', open it without delay. Your life will never be the same again. It won't ruin you, but it could make your spiritual fortune. The real things of value consist not of *physical assets* but of *spiritual values – love is the highest.*

Keeping in God's love

One of the underlying foundational aspects of trusting God in adversity is found in Jude 1:21, where we are told to 'keep ourselves in the love of God', because we can obviously take ourselves out. The instruction is given to ensure that we keep in mind the possibility that we can remove ourselves from the influence of His love. It isn't that God ceases to love us. Rather we, forgetful of favour, can wander into a foreign field like the prodigal son – not so blatant or so rebellious perhaps; but to be away one inch is the same as being as far away as a yard. The Hebrews writer says this, 'Therefore we must give the more earnest heed to the things we have heard, lest we drift away.'[233] To slip or drift means to flow by or to carelessly pass – hence, to miss.

As we slumber on the riverbank in the height of summer, the moored boat slips its rope, and the current takes it silently downstream; we never noticed. This is what can happen in the Christian life. The Bible doesn't waste words. This command, for command it is, is there because it could happen. It is both an encouragement and a warning. It's an encouragement because it is possible to so keep ourselves from slipping along the bank and a warning because it is also possible to succumb to its peril. When in the midst of suffering or trial, we can also let slip the things of God because of anger and perturbation.

We *put* ourselves in God's love when we understand the nature of God's love, and we *keep* ourselves in that love of God when we embrace a cross. That is what God's love is all about. Perhaps it is now that we begin to lose our readers! Pain, anguish, and suffering can do little to teach, but 'tears', said Henry Ward Beecher 'are telescopes.' Through tears, we look at God. Through them, we begin to appreciate the value, necessity, and utter outpouring of God's heart to us. When we begin to highly value the Cross, we are sure to keep ourselves within the ambit of that great overflowing love.

Hosea, the Old Testament prophet, depicts a story of selfless love. His suffering in personal life, told with frankness, reveals the love of the eternal heart of God. He went after the wife of his youth, who had left him for other men until sold into slavery as some chattel. He bought her back in the marketplace, brought her home, and loved her still. God has such patience with us. If Hosea could love Gomer like that, couldn't God do likewise with humankind? For isn't the best in humanity rooted there by God?

Every time a person repents and comes to faith, God remembers Calvary. It is never far from His heart. In the Old Testament he speaks thus: 'Ephraim, how can I give you up? Israel, how can I let you go?'[234] He cannot, for He has pledged Himself. How can God let us go when He has spent so much on our salvation? There is a hymn that was often sung in my youth, 'O Love That Wilt Not Let Me Go.' Its second line reads, 'I rest my weary soul in Thee.'[235] If God won't let us go, can we let Him Go – when we remember Calvary? The refrain of another hymn says this:

Lest I forget Gethsemane,
Lest I forget Thine agony;
Lest I forget Thy love for me,
Lead me to Calvary.[236]

The first aspect to keeping ourselves in the love of God is to *perceive the greatness* of His unselfish unconditional love for us. We illustrate that we have done so when we grasp and surrender to God's plan. Commenting about the rapid gains of religion around the world, A. W. Tozer, an Amercian pastor and preacher said, 'But the alarming thing is that our gains are mostly external and our losses are wholly internal; and since it is the *quality* of our religion that is affected by internal conditions, it may be that our supposed gains are but losses spread over a wider field.'[237] Our faith, recorded at Calvary, is more than an adherence to a set of rules. It is a 'new creature' in

Christ. God uses circumstances to render us *perfect*, to create His own identity in us. He is out to test our radical trust – so that whatever and whenever, we 'keep ourselves in the love of God.' Often, we cannot connect God to the real circumstances of life, and we question the reality of suffering with the heart of love we have read about. To lie still in the Calvary-gashed hand of God is an awesome experience and teaches us trust in extremity.

A cross is something we choose. His plan and purpose for us, He chooses. His choices seem strange to us and, at times, terrifying. The place where champions are made is the place of complete trust in His will for us! All that humanity searches for, unless it be associated with God, will crumble and pass. Solomon, the wisest man on earth, could well say, 'I have seen all the works that are done under the sun; and indeed, all is vanity and grasping for the wind.'[238] Nothing we do will last unless it is underwritten by God. Our walk is often on sand, and the waves of time flow over and wash it all away. Work for God is wrought in granite and will stand in eternity.

We tend to judge God by how we feel. If we feel good and our circumstances stroke us, then God is good, and we are right on the button. But, if they are contrary, and we feel bad, we believe that God is judging us for past misdemeanours! We mistake the process for the end. God is looking at the whole picture. He is looking at a bride 'without spot or wrinkle'.[239] Earthly executives prepare plans and execute programmes without reference to men and women on the shop floor because senior managers are paid for that expertise. The people on the workforce often misunderstand the decision. But in the end, the managers' plan works for them, bringing them a greater dividend.

We all have to make decisions in our lives that are fashioned by our hearts rather than perceived by our intellect. We need to recognise that God knows what he's about. Often we don't think He does because we are confused by the physical evidence. The facts somehow do not add up. *They never will*! God deals not in facts but in faith. When we surrender to His will, we keep ourselves in His love because, by doing so, we acknowledge that He loves us endlessly.

We take ourselves out of God's love when things go contrary. But we are told, 'Look upon every man, woman, or child who tries your patience or angers you as a means of grace to humble you.'[240] We take ourselves out of the love of Christ when we resort to human discontent and anger. 'Love bears all things.'[241] Surrender means that God doesn't bargain. He states what He wants and expects it. Our problem is that we want to stay in control; to be submissive is not natural but supernatural. We all have preconceived ideas about role functions for other people and expect those around us to conform to that perception. If not, we manipulate to ensure they do.

We take ourselves out of God's love when things go well. Spiritual growth occurs only when we are willing to co-operate with God in our circumstances, good or bad. When in the good times, we often don't know what to do. The wisest thing, and therefore the best thing, is to do what we do when circumstances are contrary. We hang on to God, pray without ceasing, extol His name in the darkness, and generally draw near to God. Keep doing that; it will help prevent pride and passivity.

We take ourselves out of God's love when we are too busy. How busy is too busy? Who will tell me? He will! I need to learn the art of leaving things undone. Because of the stress of the unfinished, the art of leaving things undone is a *learned* art! Whether it be housework, raising children, church work, or work in the secular marketplace, there is no end to the jobs that need to be done. Yet I've found that, even though there is a world to be won, God expects me to first attend to the mission field between my own two feet!

We put ourselves in *the love of God when we live in an atmosphere where love can blossom.* Truth is the ground of love, and we need to constantly ask ourselves important questions – questions that sift our motives. Integrity is the structure we build on truth, and the great need of our lives is to honestly and without partiality seek to know where we stand in relation to our attitudes and motives. The Bible is replete with enquiry, as the Lord searches individuals, asking short but pithy and life-changing questions. What he does not ask we should. We need to keep a checklist to keep us in the love of God and not in our own self-love. God can ask the shortest but hardest question. God came to Cain and asked, 'Why are you angry? And why is your countenance fallen?'[242] He asked a depressed Elijah, 'What are you doing here?'[243] To Judas, He said this: 'Friend, why have you come?'[244] To Peter, He said, 'Do you really love me more than a these?'[245] And of Saul, He asked, 'Why are you persecuting me?'[246]

The more we concentrate on ourselves, the more likely we are to take ourselves out of God's love. The basic discipline of examining ourselves with soul-searching questions will bring to the surface gold or flotsam. Our life is a quest to seek approval, and although we might never confess that desire, it does dog our footsteps. Adam and Eve lost favour in the Garden of Eden, and humankind has unconsciously sought it ever since. If people do not get approval from God, they will seek it from other people to bolster their self-image. Life then becomes a process of striving for recognition.

Athletes and footballers get their reward from the crowd, entertainers from the audience, and pastors from the congregation (possibly!). But in essence, the only approval that matters is God's. 'Well done thou good and faithful servant.'[247] I decorated my late wife's sewing room, and it was pleasing to hear her say, 'That's nice.' Her approval made the work worthwhile. I was working to please her.

I'm also living to please God. Hear the psalmist: 'Bless the Lord, O my soul; and all that is within me, bless His holy name!'[248] My whole heart and being seeking God – all that is within seeks all that which is without. Paul says, 'Keep the unity of the Spirit.'[249] And similarly, we are admonished in these various passages: 'Keep yourself pure.'[250] 'Keep oneself unspotted from the world.'[251] 'Keep yourselves from idols.'[252] If we keep ourselves in the love of God, all these other commandments will be fulfilled.

An allegory – A dog called Oscar: Such love is startling

A dog called Oscar had as his friend a white cat called Arthur; the two were constant companions. One day, Arthur died, and his owner buried him in the back garden. Next morning, he awoke to find Oscar curled up beside Arthur in the same basket where they always slept. It seems that Oscar had gone out through the dog flap, dug up the cat, dragged him back to the house through the dog flap, put him in the basket and licked him clean, and then fallen asleep exhausted. It was quite a feat, for Arthur was a huge cat and used to help Oscar climb onto the sofa. The two animals were inseparable.

Oscar now has a new friend, a small kitten called Limpet.

We had two miniature schnauzers, who shared a large basket. And Cadbury, our chocolate-point Siamese cat, used to sneak up and climb in the basket as the two dogs settled down to sleep. The three were clearly friends, and when Schweppes died, Fritz, her brother, searched the garden, under every bush and tree trying to find her. He clearly missed her and became pensive at her disappearance. But she was not buried in the garden!

Friendship, even in the animal realm, is heart-moving and wonderful. And it can sometimes be a rare thing among humans. If you have one friend, you are rich. Many are the quotations from philosophers and famous people on friendship. 'Books, like friends, should be few and well chosen, said Samuel Paterson. And in 1537, Pietro Aretino wrote, 'I keep my friends as misers do their treasure, because, of all the things granted us by wisdom, none is greater or better than friendship.' It was Len Wein who said, 'A true friend is someone who is there for you when he'd rather be anywhere else.' And the Bible comes to our aid with this saying: 'An honest answer is the sign of true friendship.'[253]

I am sure that Jesus has a greater love for me than Oscar had for Arthur and Cadbury had for Fritz and Schweppes, and, speaking reverentially, on Calvary, He ensured I was licked clean! 'Greater love has no one than this that he lay down his life for his friends. I no longer call you servants, because a servant does not know his master's business. Instead, I have called you friends, for everything that I learned from my Father I have made known to you.'[254] What a great friendship! Aren't you glad Jesus is our friend?

The maiden in the Song of Songs says, 'He is my friend.' He is the friend to all those who call upon Him. 'A man who has friends must himself be friendly, but there is a friend who sticks closer than a brother.'[255] He sticks to us through thick and thin, as they say – through the ups and downs of living in all the complex vagaries and deviations of tumultuous trials and opposition.

He knows all about us, and yet He is still our friend; that is the mark of true friendship. We cannot hide anything from Him. We are open books, which he can read effortlessly. But for all our faults and shortcomings, he is still our friend. As Charles Peguy said, 'Love is rarer than genius itself. And friendship is rarer than love.' That is a strong saying; love and friendship must be present in a marriage, for if it is just love, then love can fail, for it could be lust. To make a bond like that work, it must include friendship. It was Dag Hammarskjold who said, 'Friendship needs no words." The silence of marriage is exactly that, or it should be.

The climax of friendship love is to die for the other. Lip love is proved suspect if it is disinclined to forfeit life itself. But Jesus is no such fraud; he not only died, but in his resurrection, he also showered us with underserved grace. Jonathan risked death to assemble with David. Jesus not only risked death; he went under the murky waters of the grave so that we might partake of that crystal flowing river. Our value is estimated by our worth to God, and that worth is confirmed by the death of His only son. We are very valuable to God. When trials come, as they will, remember that. His love is limitless and too deep to understand. And He constantly surprises us with His searching faithfulness.

Chapter 12

Seven Fat Years

Surely there is an end or future, and your hope will not be cut off.
—Proverbs 23:18

Joseph interpreted Pharaoh's dream of seven fat and seven lean years and made provision for the famine. In our home situation many years ago, we had passed through seven very lean and horrendous years. Patricia's life was a physical misery and I was working all hours to make the never-ending ends meet – looking after her, running a church, and attending to the needs of my children. *Lean* was an underestimate of our situation.

Unknown to me, Patricia had just spoken to God. She had asked if He could please reverse our bad fortune and, instead of seven lean years, give us seven fat years and had left it in His almighty hands. The next day, a Baptist minister I remotely knew turned up on our doorstep and said God had sent him to pray for her. I was away at work, lecturing at that time. He said, 'I the Lord have seen your seven lean years, and now I will give you seven fat years.' Without doubt, you could say that this blessing was a prophetic word in season. Whichever way you look at it, the minister didn't know our situation or my wife's specific prayer. She mentioned it when I got home, and we waited expectantly and, I suppose, somewhat apprehensively.

Very soon afterwards, my mother-in-law was visiting our home. She asked how long my rear garden was. As I didn't know, I measured it. And as I did so, I looked over the rear fence and saw the road that passed. Immediately, now knowing the length and seeing the road, an idea came to me: *I can build another house on my plot with access.*

I applied to the Birmingham Planning Department, submitted the plans, and received permission, which caused a furore in the neighbourhood. I lived on a road that was like an open-ended cul-de-sac. Many of the residents were connected to the famous King Edward's Camp Hill Grammar School, which was opposite. It was like an old boys' association. One was the head of the Birmingham Science Museum, another was a professor of medicine at Queen Elizabeth Hospital, and my immediate neighbour was director of the Cater's News Agency. The latter always vetted all planning applications but was absent when mine fell across his desk! The neighbours committed such a protest that the planning department rescinded the application and paid me compensation, which paid off my mortgage. Everyone was disenchanted with me, but I got the money, and God was on the move.

A few years later, we moved to Solihull following the call of God. There, I joined my younger brother's church as his associate. Solihull is on the outskirts of Birmingham, and we bought a bungalow. As I sat in the solicitor's office, he looked at the plan and said, 'You have a building plot in your back garden.' It was a corner site, and the land was about a third of an acre. I asked my new neighbours about building there, and they assured me I would never get permission; someone had already tried and had been refused. Even the electricity board had tried and failed. But nothing deterred me, as I knew that God was on my side. I designed a bungalow specifically for that site, sent in the application, and received permission. I sold the land, paid off my mortgage, and was able to go to London, under God's call, with a good sum in the bank towards a new home in the capital. God knew several years before I did that I would move to London, and He was making provision for that day.

Correspondingly, Patricia's health began to improve. And as the seven years passed, we moved to the London Borough of Harrow. For the first time in a long time, she was able to go out and about freely and eat in restaurants, and that was indeed a miracle. Both tubes were eventually removed, and life was almost normal. Because we had always put God first in every aspect of our lives, He took care of us in so many ways that it would take another book to explain them fully. We sowed into His kingdom with time, money, and energy, and we reaped eventually of His benefits. He is no man's debtor. The seven fat years were not about just financial reward but also about quality of life itself. There is roundness about God; he covers all aspects in his grace. Ministry opened up for me, and I entered a phase of life undreamt of and certainly not expected.

The 'seven years' prophetic forecast was by the minister in answer to prayer, lasted four times that length. Let us remember that God can turn the seven lean years into many years of plenty. He does indeed own the cattle on a thousand hills and the wealth in every mine. But also remember that 'wealth' need not be cash! *Health is better than dollars.*

God's favour

There are, no doubt, many among the righteous who regularly attend God's house, participate in corporate prayer, and diligently conduct home worship, and yet their faithfulness may seem somewhat in vain, as they wait for God's ultimate favour on their lives. At the weekly services, they tarry in expectation of a special visitation or revelation from God's word or possible encouragement in the unity of worship or perhaps a spoken word from a colleague. *Is this or will this be their hour?*

Some who know the sonship of salvation live as servants, feeling the condemnation of the law, although set free by grace. Rather than walking in the glorious liberty of the sons of God, they stumble in hesitant freedom, failing to live in the privileges promised at Calvary. But we know that the living word is adamant: 'and because you are sons, God has sent forth the Spirit of His Son into our hearts, crying, "Abba! Father!" Therefore, you are no longer a slave, but a son; and if a son, then an heir through God.'[256] Therefore, our text affirms, at some God-designed time. 'Surely...our hope will not be cut off.'[257] The future is safe in his favoured hands.

What then is our expectation?

'My soul, wait silently upon God; for my expectation is from him.'[258] Our expectation is not from humankind, no matter how influential and powerful, but *only* from God. Firstly, our expectation is of sins forgiven and all that means in practical and spiritual benefits. God sees me as he sees His son, righteous. We cannot be more righteous; we are as clean as Jesus. If God were to look at us in our own righteousness, all he would see is sin, guilt, and pollution. But casting aside all our own worth, we stand in Christ alone; he then sees the sacrifice and the blood of Calvary and pronounces us clean.

We received not only pardon and justifying righteousness but also *adopted privileges*, for we are now his children. 'Among whom also we all once conducted ourselves in the lusts of our flesh, fulfilling the desires of the flesh and of the mind, and were by nature children of wrath,[259] just as the others.'[260] But our newborn sonship admits us to his house, not as domestics or servants but sons. We sit at His table and have constant access to His august presence. 'He brought me to the banqueting-house, and his banner over me was love.'[261]

We have peace in death, not joy, although some will have that. The process of death can be slow and painful, but the Bible says, 'Mark the perfect man, and behold the upright: for the end of that man is peace.'[262] We can know in death glory in eternity, which is a sure promise and provision: 'But now having been set free from sin, and having become slaves of God, you have your fruit to holiness, and the end, *everlasting life*.'[263] Life will start in eternity, which is the reality of salvation. This life on earth is but a stepping stone to the glories that are to come. 'And every one that hath forsaken houses, or brethren, or sisters, or father, or mother, or wife, or children, or lands, for my name's sake, shall receive a hundredfold, and shall *inherit everlasting life.*'[264] [Italics added]

We are, therefore, heirs: 'And if children, then heirs; heirs of God, and joint-heirs with Christ.'[265] This is part of our father's last will and testament that cannot be broken (John 17). We have an inheritance voiced by Christ; we are entitled by sonship and His sacrifice. Therefore, He can bestow this gift on us, and will share with his children. 'He shall see the travail of His soul, and be satisfied. By His knowledge my righteous Servant shall justify many, for He shall bear their iniquities.'[266] Being 'joint-heirs with Christ' we have riches abundant – riches of humility, holiness, grace, and eventually glory. We must fix our eyes on present privileges that the gospel has provided.

The assurance of expectation

At the commencement of this chapter we said 'Surely there is a future,' and so there is. Some are but 'babes in Christ,[267] and see men as 'trees walking',[268] but we have been given the first fruits of assurance and expectation by the Holy Spirit: 'Who has also sealed us, and given the earnest of the Spirit in our hearts.'[269] The engagement ring of promise is ours. We are betrothed to Christ; the contract has been sealed. There is no longer any doubt; our names are written in the Lamb's book of life.[270] We may not fully understand the process of adoption, but gradually, over time, our eyes will see the glory of God manifest in failing flesh. And failing it might be, as trials and terrors encompass our footsteps, but our leanness can become richness in material and spiritual avenues.

Increasingly, we become aware of holy desires, which are contrary to our nature, for we were born in sin and inherited from Adam our rebellious nature. We, therefore, glory not in our change because the change is brought about by God's Spirit. We do not and cannot claim glory in our maturity. It is of God, or we have no real salvation. Salvation is of God, not of the creature so blessed. Its success is in the blood of Christ; its influence is by the Holy Spirit, and its development, by the love of God. The Trinity combines to pledge eternal reassurance.

Whatever comes, we have this assurance

The authority of God's word is sufficient to counteract all dispossessions and failings. If we consider indwelling sin, the word states, 'For sin shall not be your master, because you are not under law, but under grace.'[271] He will subdue those raging passions so that our expectation is not cut off. When we consider Satan and his power we read, 'And the God of peace will crush Satan under your feet shortly.'[272] So what of the world that reviles and rejects us as it did Him? 'No weapon formed against you shall prosper, and every tongue which rises against you in judgment you shall condemn. This is the heritage of the servants of the LORD, says the LORD.'[273] This threefold support assuages doubts and raises our expectation in God. Our text says, 'Surely there will be an end' – an end of doubt, despair, danger, and conflict. And although we see through a 'glass darkly',[274] we shall see beyond the misty horizon. For we know that 'all things work together for those who love God'.[275] We know that all tears will be wiped away, and night will be turned glorious day. As the old hymn quoted by William Jay says:

> Then shall we see, and taste, and know
> All we desire or wish below
> And every power find sweet employ,
> In that eternal world of joy.

Our testimony proves that God listens and is on our case.

It was evening, and I was standing in my hall and opening the morning post. One envelope contained a bill I had forgotten in the midst of the daily routine. It was far more than I could pay. It was not rash spending by just forgetfulness, a misjudgement. I prayed there and then and offered it to God, and a knock came on my door. There stood a man and asked if I wanted to sell the Austin A40 on my drive.

It was my wife's car, but she could no longer drive it as the muscles in her eyes had badly deteriorated. I had intended selling it at some time. I asked what the man would give, and his offer was the same as the amount of the bill in my hand! God says, 'Before you call I will answer.'[276] And so he did. Leanness to provision is God's speciality.

I was tinkering with the thermostat on my Ford Corsair and spoke to my wife in the inner hall from our front doorstep. I told her I was going to see our neighbour to borrow an adjustable spanner, so I could finish installing the new thermostat. 'I've left mine at work, I added, 'but please pray for another car, for this one is failing fast.' My neighbour invited me into his garage. He went to the drawer that held the spanner and turned and asked if I wanted to buy his car, a Vauxhall FE range two-litre with 22,000 miles on the clock. Whenever it rained, he dried it and put it in the garage. It was in perfect showroom condition. All he wanted was £800 and that was just the amount I had in my account. Patricia's prayer was answered in five minutes – pretty good I think!

Chapter 13

Keep Calm and Carry On

In spring 1939, an anonymous civil servant was entrusted with finding suitable slogans for propaganda posters intended to comfort, inspire, and stiffen public resolve, should the massed armies of Nazi Germany ever cross the Channel. Three were designed, and two were produced. The first read, 'Your Courage, Your Cheerfulness, Your Resolution Will Bring Us Victory.' The second, identically styled, stated, 'Freedom is in Peril.' This was during the period of heavy bombing and anticipated gas attacks. More than a million of these flyers were printed from August onwards, and both posters began appearing all over the country, on billboards, in shops, and on railway platforms.

The third was held back. This one was for the real crisis – *invasion*. A few may have made their way on to select officials' walls, but the vast majority of the British public never saw it. This poster enjoined: 'Keep Calm and Carry On.' Now, suddenly, it's everywhere, from homes to pubs to government offices. The Lord Chamberlain's Office at Buckingham Palace, the Prime Minister's strategy unit at No 10, the Serious Fraud Office, the US embassy in Belgium, the office of the vice chancellor of Cambridge University, the Emergency Planning Office at Nottingham council, and the officers' mess in Basra have all ordered posters. It even hangs in my daughter's new kitchen.

For sixty years, this poster had been forgotten. Then one day in 2000, Stuart Manley, co-owner with his wife, Mary, of Barter Books in Alnwick, Northumberland, was sifting through a box of hardbacks he had bought at auction when he saw, 'a big piece of paper folded up at the bottom.' He explains, 'I opened it out, and I thought, wow. That's quite something. I showed it to Mary, and she agreed. So we framed it and put it up on the bookshop wall. And that's where it all started.'[277]

Today, you can buy Keep Calm and Carry On mugs, doormats, T-shirts, hoodies, cufflinks, baby clothes, and flight bags from any number of retailers. You can use the design as a screensaver for your computer or mobile phone. There are facsimiles of the poster itself, which Barter Books initially reproduced after a rash of customers asked to buy its copy (one offered £1,000). They have sold tens of thousands of them.

Alain Samson, a social psychologist at the London School of Economics, says that in times of difficulty, 'People are brought together by looking for common values or purposes, symbolized by the crown and the message of resilience. The words are also particularly positive, reassuring, in a period of uncertainty, anxiety, even perhaps of cynicism.'

Dr Lesley Prince, who lectures in social psychology at Birmingham University, is blunter still. 'It is a quiet, calm, authoritative voice of reason,' he says. 'It's not about British stiff upper lip, really. The point is that people have been sold a lie since the 1970s. They were promised the earth and now they're worried about everything – their jobs, their homes, their bank, their money, their pension. This is saying, look, somebody out there knows what's going on, and it'll be all right.'

There is no doubt that we are living in a morally decaying country. I have probably seen the best of Britain in my lifetime. I passed through the war years of privation as a young child and witnessed victory when I was ten. The forties and fifties were struggling years, as people came to terms with peace again, passing through the hunt for post-war jobs, the re-establishment of homes, and the consequent baby boom. Many soldiers could not cope with peace. They were traumatised by constant noise and killing. After discharge, they had no need to follow orders or face danger and lived in a resultant vacuum of inaction.

Many lives and marriages were wrecked, and although the nation eventually recovered economically through the seventies to nineties, I doubt if it will ever recover from the loss of manhood. Some of our finest minds were spread across the unploughed fields of Europe. Succeeding political generations have wilted under global pressure, and we are left with a poor imitation of real quality; it has been replaced by greed, lying, spin doctoring, and manipulation. No wonder the populace displays the wartime poster. Keep Calm and Carry On. What else can they do? There is another war raging that too few notice; it is a war for truth.

The nation could turn to God as it did in the war years, but even He has now been sidelined, as humanism, materialism, and atheism have mainly overcome in public life, basic Christian belief. Those of us who still pray beseech God, asking for His Spirit to send a true revival that reaches into the governing segment of our society. In Israel, it was said, 'For the leaders of this people cause them to err.'[278] This is true of the last decade, where money has replaced the true value of character. Real values have become disorientated by greed. Convenience and cunning subterfuge have tarnished the quality gold of character.[279] In addition, any form of trial is viewed as coming from an angry God who fails to understand us. We judge God by human standards and believe he exists to simply bless us. The social state has misrepresented God by their acts of charity; in other words, God is there to make us happy.

Calmness is the gift of God and the endowment to those who put their trust in Him. It is quality that suggests the person has a gold lining to their souls, and God will have gold in our lives so we had better keep calm and carry on. In fact, that is the motive of the Christian life. The frenzy of life is mollified by His great and gracious hand, and He leads us onward through thick and thin to the ultimate reality. His is a peace that passes human understanding and a joy unspeakable and full of glory.

Gold has been a highly sought-after precious metal for jewellery, for sculpture, and for ornamentation and for barter and exchange since the beginning of recorded history. Gold is dense, soft, shiny, and the most malleable and ductile pure metal known, and it remains so, without rusting in air or water. Gold dissolves only in mercury but is insoluble in nitric acid, which will dissolve silver and base metals. This is exploited as the basis of the gold refining technique known as 'inquartation and parting'. Nitric acid has long been used to confirm the presence of gold in items, and this is the origin of the colloquial term *acid test*, referring to a *gold standard* test for genuine value. God sets out to ensure that we pass the 'acid test,' that we are the unadulterated and real article.

'When you were born, you cried and the world rejoiced. Let the rest of your life be in such a fashion so that when you die, the world cries and you rejoice.'[280] There is a word in Lamentations 4:1 that says, 'How the gold has lost its lustre, the fine gold become dull.' The glittering gold resplendent in its polished value has become dim, such that it is noticeable, or why else would the writer mention it? How like our lives, which become such that they lose their appeal. As Christians, we are expected to keep the brightness burnished and the glitter bright. The Apostle John says, 'I counsel you to buy from me gold refined in the fire.'[281] We are not admonished only to possess it but to polish it – polish it in the everyday concourse of life.

So many treasures remain hidden in the antique shop of time because the gold has been neglected. Good testimonies rich in heritage often lay among the jumbled trash of littered lives that amount to little. The world will never lament us, for it never knew us. The gold bangle that should have adorned the slender wrist of some great personage is left untouched because it lacked lustre.

Wedding rings are made from gold, and so are God's people, especially leaders. The preciousness of the metal confirms the value of the gift, and in leaders, the trace element that runs through their lives is precious gold, white gold. Leaders are not made; they are born – born not with a silver spoon in their mouth but with a golden lining to their soul. They shine at something and shine through the darkened lanes of adversity.

Unfortunately, as time passes, the gold can become stained and unrecognisable, usually through neglect. Therefore, the question to ask is this: Will the world cry, and you rejoice? Or will we lose our reward[282] while the world fails to notice the bargain, as it lies huddled among the paste jewellery? 'Do you see a man who excels in his work? He will stand before kings.'[283] The excelling is in the polishing! Daily, the vicissitudes grind against the roughness of our lives, making it smooth and glossy. This makes us more refined, elegant, and complete. Life is full of grit, and its marks wear upon us until we become resplendent to His glory.

The purity of gold is measured by the term *fineness*, which defines gold content in parts per thousand. For instance, a gold nugget containing 885 parts of pure gold and 115 parts of other metals, such as silver and copper, would be 885-fine. *Karat* indicates the proportion of solid gold in an alloy based on a total of 24 parts. Thus, 14-karat gold indicates a composition of gold and 10 parts of other metals – 14K gold is usually used in good quality jewellery manufacture.

So many of us are composite Christians, part gold and part other metals. I was once in a shop in Singapore that belonged to an elder of the Church of Resurrection and was run by Canon James Hong. The elder invited me to buy anything in the shop, and he would give me a good deal – I had preached on Sunday, and no doubt he had been touched by the Word. I looked around for the smallest item I could and saw a small, square, thin watch in the corner of a cabinet, the size of an after-dinner chocolate mint. 'How much?' I asked.

He replied that it was the most expensive item in the shop. He told me it was worth $300, which I baulked at. And I said I'd leave it.

Throughout that week, I called in, and the elder and I bartered over that watch. Eventually I agreed to the price. On returning home, I had it valued. It was an 18K gold 'flagship' piece by Logines, top of the line, worth £2,500 then and now about £5,500. That was about thirty years ago. I have since given the watch to my elder son. I did not use it, as the winding nob was too small for my big fingers. It does not have any use hidden away and is better on display. Too many Christians are 18K quality gold in God but are hidden away because of some minor deficiency or because they have lost their lustre. Gold does not need a lot of attention, but it does need *some* attention.

In the letter to Laodicea, the Apostle John describes God's concern over the church. This is the only church about which John writes no praise. And in doing that, he showed how God views the soul that lives in a state of tepidity. It should make us wary about allowing our lives to sink into a similar state. Therefore, they were encouraged to, 'Buy [earn or gain] Gold tried in the fire.'[284] They thought they were rich, but they were poor, although the Laodicea church was prosperous.

In the Bible, the refined character of a person is implicitly referred to as possessing gold. 'With your blood you purchased men for God from every tribe and language and people and nation.'[285] Christ earned our freedom by His sacrifice on Calvary, in that His death secured our salvation. Thus, to buy gold is to live a sacrificial life – to die daily and yet live in glory. 'For I think that God hath set forth us, the apostles last, as it were appointed to death: for we are made a spectacle unto the world, and to angels, and to men.'[286] They played on the theatre of this world before angels, demons, and humankind, who were examining their conduct resulting from forgiveness and rebirth. Was their character gold?

You notice the difference between 'you say' and 'you are' (in verse 17]. *You say* you are rich, but *you are* poor. The citizens of Laodicea were rich; and they knew it! They were unbearable. Even the church people manifested this same proud, defiant, conceited attitude. They were poor, naked, and blind. To answer this, God calls them *to buy* His gold, *to clothe* themselves with His raiment, and lastly *to anoint* their eyes with His eye salve.

Peter states that the gold to be purchased from God is faith tried in the fire. 'These [trials] have come so that your faith – of greater worth than gold, which perishes even though refined by fire – may be proved genuine and may result in praise, glory and honour when Jesus Christ is revealed.'[287] Job, passing through his trials, echoes the same thought: 'But He knows the way that I take; when He has tested me, I shall come forth as gold.'[288] Solomon in all his wisdom recounts life and quotes: 'The refining pot is for silver and the furnace for gold, but the LORD tests the hearts.'[289]

Tests are necessary for life, and we all will go through them. God is not a sadist who delights in our pain, but the only way to prove who we are is the spiritual acid test. Several years ago my first wife and I were in America and came across a pamphlet that described pain. It showed a picture of ten faces, the first one depicting no pain (smiling) and the final one with in pain. The facial expressions changed from happiness to great sadness, in fact anguish. The first was minimum; the tenth was maximum. Between that table, you chose the level. You could then explain to the doctor what pain you were in, and he would understand. You could use this man-made list to talk to God!

If you feel you are on the treadmill of life or facing the acid test, remember that God's intention is to bring you to perfection – to make you the authentic product. He went through the ultimate test of Calvary, from which you are exempt. God says he will not test us beyond our ability to bear. If we were the first on the pain scale all our life, we would have little value. Jesus had many faces when on earth, and now when he looks at us with compassion. His desire is for our best – you'd better believe it.

The Haka is a traditional ancestral war cry, dance, or challenge of the Maori people of New Zealand. It is a posture dance performed by a group, with vigorous movements and stamping of feet. Traditionally, it is performed by the All Blacks International Rugby Team and Kiwis Rugby Team. Te Rauparaha composed Ka Mate in 1820 as a celebration of life over death after his fortunate escape from pursuing Ngati Maniapoto and Waikato enemies. He had hidden from them in a food storage pit and climbed back into the light to be met by a chief friendly to him, Te Whareangi (the 'hairy man').

Various actions are employed in the course of the Haka performance. Facial contortions include the performers showing the whites of their eyes and poking out of their tongues. And a wide variety of vigorous body actions include slapping the hands against the body and the stamping of feet. All the while, the performers chant words, and a variety of cries and grunts are used. Haka may be understood as a kind of symphony in which the different parts of the body represent many instruments. The hands, arms, legs, feet, voice, eyes, tongue, and the body as a whole combine to express courage, annoyance, joy, and other feelings relevant to the purpose of the occasion.

In former times, the *peruperu* was performed before a battle to invoke the god of war and to discourage and frighten the enemy. If the Haka was not performed in total unison, this was regarded as a bad omen for the battle. These are the last two lines: 'Step upward, another step upward! A step upward, another...the Sun shines!"

Those who performed the Ka Mate won. Before the game started, they did their dance, chanted, and performed actions, much to the pleasure of the home crowd. The performance was in unison, and on the field the rugby team was in unison – they won. Psalm 133 says, 'Where the brethren dwell together in unity, there the Lord commands the blessing' or secures the victory. Sometimes what's important is not the outstanding skill of an individual player (although this is desired) but that the team moves as one.

I once worked for Wates, the large building and civil engineering contractor. The agent on one particular contract told me of a man the company had had to exclude from the shuttering team because he was too good. He was an excellent carpenter, far better than any other on the team. But that made him a threat. He no doubt also thought of himself as too good, and so he was. His removal and replacement liberated the other men to work without the distraction of inferiority. Their vertical speed increased as they went up the building, floor after floor. Targets were reached, bonuses were paid, and everyone was happy. The skilled man went onto other things, and he was also liberated by not being confined to mundane operations.

The words of the Ka Mate are also significant if applied to Christian things. 'Step upward, and another step upward! A step upward, another...the Sun shines.' We, as pilgrims of the faith, are called to walk with God, upward, and another step upward. And so it goes every day until the sun shines. The Old Testament comes to our aid in a disguise: 'The king of Israel had said to his officials, "Don't you know that Ramoth Gilead belongs to us and yet we are doing nothing to retake it from the king of Aram?"'[290] The word Ramoth means 'heights', and in Christ there are heights of daily ascent. We take one step at a time to come up from the pit (like Te Rauparaha ascending from the food storage pit). And we reach the heights of peace, joy, power, and victory. Well can we sing a Haka, in holy words of triumph, declaring that we shall overcome our adversary. God's reward for faithful lives – faithful through trial and adversity – is first a unified body corporate as one with our brethren. And next, He lifts our praise until the sun of His righteousness cascades upon us. Oh *yes!*

Chapter 14

Chusssh, Chusssh, Chusssh

A British scientist has developed a new sound that could revolutionise mobile telephones and safety alarms. The sound was demonstrated a year or two back, and as a result, already thirty countries have made a request for more information. Professor Deborah Withington of Leeds University said, 'I believe it's not only a world-beating British invention, but it's going to save thousands of lives every year.'[291] Anyone hearing the broadband sound should know the precise location of its source. The invention came about because Professor Withington was sitting in her car when she heard a fire engine's siren but could not tell which direction it was coming from. Because of that, she knew she was in possible danger. 'It was a eureka moment.' Apparently, conventional 'sinusoidal' waves confuse the ear by seeming to come from many points. The new 'white noise' wave uses multiple-frequency analysis, clarifying the source of the noise.

It initiates a reaction that makes anyone instantly turn towards that sound. Withington has selected sounds for electronic engineers, which she knows the human brain will recognise and interpret within milliseconds. They then convert them into electronic noises, which, according to need, are variations on *chusssh, chusssh, chusssh*. Hearers of the sound are virtually unable to resist turning their face to the direction of the sound.

This phenomenon was demonstrated on television recently. A series of people were asked to walk down a corridor, and the sound was turned on just as they entered security camera range. They all turned and looked and were all caught on camera. None could resist. Because of this, banks, large department stores and single shops are now evaluating the possibility and potential of installation of *chusssh, chusssh, chusssh* sound-activated cameras on their premises.

It could also rid everyday life of one of those embarrassing moments when everyone in a room (except, of course those without phones – happy people) searches for his or her mobile phone when one rings. Building workers, especially tunnel builders, would benefit because often reversing lorries cannot be re-orientated. Reversing alarms were invented fifty-one years ago in Japan. But now, not only lorries but cars as well could be enabled, thus preventing accidents involving children. Withington's sound could also assist greatly in the event of a fire, so that people caught in dense smoke could be guided round corners towards escape routes and exits.

Here then is a noise that causes people to turn towards its source. We read of a similar sound in scripture: 'And suddenly there came a sound from heaven, as of a rushing mighty wind, and it filled the whole house where they were sitting.'[292] When this happened, there was a result in the city. The sound was accompanied by results. 'And when this sound occurred, the multitude came together, and were confused, because everyone heard them speak in his own language.'[293] They were not confused about the sound but about the multiplicity of languages. This sound from heaven changed things, drawing people towards it. They knew the source of the sound – heaven. It was directional. It was God's *chusssh, chusssh, chusssh*.

John, the disciple, would often lay his head on Jesus' breast; he liked the sound of God's heartbeat, metaphorically speaking, for it is a noise that causes people to turn towards its source. It identifies him and saves us. Through trials and anxiety, we can just lie upon the divine bosom and draw strength in our helplessness. It is deep answering unto deep, like a newborn child on its mother's breast. God tells us that even if we do recognise the sound from heaven, we still know almost nothing of His greatness. Even the whispers could blind us with revelation. God hid Moses with His hand as he passed by; God's glory was too great to be seen. Sunglasses are essential for a closer walk with God.

Whispers and edges

'Indeed these are the mere edges of His ways, and how small a whisper we hear of Him!'[294] After a long catalogue of great deeds and personal greatness, it is said of God that, for all these public display of almightiness, we still only see the edges. And the combination of all that power is but a whisper. 'For now we see in a mirror, dimly, but then face to face. Now I know in part, but then I shall know just as I also am known.' [295] We too often stand on the fringes of life and miss God's faint whisper. He does not reveal himself fully; we have to cry with the maiden in the Song of Solomon, 'Draw me away! We will run after you…the king has brought me into his chambers.'[296]

Communication

As I sat at home one Sunday evening reading a book, Schmitz, our dog, got up from his bed and sat in front of me, looking me straight in the eye. It was a signal that he wanted something; I was not sure what and thought perhaps he wanted to go out. So I opened the back door, and he slipped out and returned to his bed. *That's it*, I thought. But in no time, he was back, sitting and looking me straight in the face again. I was nonplussed and thought perhaps he needed to go out again – possibly something he had eaten! As I walked to the door, I looked at his bowls and realised they were both empty – no food, no water. I went into the hall and looked at his other water bowl, and it was also empty. I then realised he had probably had no water since we'd left for church that morning seven hours earlier. Somehow or other I had overlooked it. His upright stance and stare were his method of communicating.

We had changed his diet to dry food, and he needed water to digest it. He had no doubt gone out into the garden to find some – possibly on leaves, for it had been raining. I filled his bowl, and he three-quarters emptied it at one go, thirsty indeed. Usually if he wanted to go out, he would sit at the door and give a small bark, just audible. His position and bark were sufficient to communicate to us that when you gotta go, you gotta go.

I like hearing children communicate, for they are uncomplicated and usually non-political. Patricia rang our daughter's six-year-old twins over Christmas one year and asked Aubrey how it had gone this year for presents. 'Magnificent,' he replied. He had been speaking to his friend the previous week and playing a game he didn't like and had been heard to say, 'I am most discontented.' Simple and direct; it couldn't be plainer.

When my wife was in a hospital in America, she communicated very clearly to the nurses who came to move her. Patricia was heard to say, 'No, no, no. Touch me, and I'll shoot you.' Her message was graphic, uncomplicated, and final. She moved at the pace and in the way that gave her the least pain. She'd had a spiral fracture of the left femur when she slipped on a piece of discarded lemon rind in a public car park. The nurses would just grasp her ankles and swing her onto or off the bed, which was, to say the least, excruciatingly painful. When I did it, it was slow and sure. We made sure both her ankles were together, and I moved them in a way she could cope with. Her hips had to be just right before movement could begin. It required clear communication without a doubt.

When I was a minister at KT in 1984, I did more counselling than I had done at HICC. I would often have someone sitting before me whose speech would wander everywhere as he or she tried to chat about the reason for the meeting. After a few minutes, I would stop them and say, 'How much do you want?' They would look surprised at my suddenness and then be embarrassed, for I had cut through the verbiage and reached the core of their dilemma. That's communication!

127

We can communicate with a word, a look, a gesture (perhaps a kiss or a squeeze of the hand), or even silence. But when God speaks his communication is *clear, concise,* and *directive.* Mary went to the resurrection garden at first light and, seeing Jesus, thought he was the gardener. But he spoke just one word – 'Mary' – and she knew it was him. He has his own method of communicating, which employs a method that suits each individual. But whatever the method, the message it paramount. The method is suited to the comprehension of whomever he is communicating with, for he knows how we each listen and understand. To Moses, a burning bush; to Paul, a flash of lightening; to Joseph, a dream; to John, a view of heaven; and to me, a text from the first chapter of Luke. 'You shall prepare a people for the Lord' that text reads. And I have done that for sixty years and will continue to do so.

Many times He has tried to communicate with me, but I was (am) too insensitive to what he wants. There were many times I didn't get it. I was too engrossed in other matters. The world beckons too loudly. We do not hear God because we hear instead the loud critical cacophony of the world. There are competing sounds. The world, the flesh, and the devil – these make up the trinity of opposition. We often tune out the divine – employing selective hearing. We hear faintly because, *being preoccupied with life,* we fail to listen.

In May 1984, I had been called to Kensington Temple. But I kept deferring my decision to leave the West Midlands and live in a London borough, thinking of the vagaries of such a conurbation, with its dense traffic and high property values. I was walking around the side of my bungalow in Solihull, pushing my lawnmower, and contemplating the impending move: Should I or shouldn't I go? Suddenly, God jumped out the shrubbery and said, 'Give it up.' Whether it was in my mind or a physical presence I do not know. All I know is that it was real – I had heard God. I left my mower where I was, walked into my bungalow, and made a phone call. All I said was, 'I'm coming.' It was a *'chusssh'* moment; of that there is no doubt. I turned my face towards God and saw my future was safe in His hands. My sick wife would not suffer for the move. It turned out the move was the best thing she could have done; the finest consultants were in London.

Our enemy has at least two hats. 'Be sober, be vigilant; because your adversary the devil, as a *roaring lion*, walketh about, seeking whom he may devour.'[297] In another scripture, we learn, 'and no marvel; for Satan himself is transformed into an *angel of light*.'[298][Italics mine] He is a roaring lion and also an angel of light. He is not a cuddly toy lion, soft and gentle, but a ferocious destroying avenger driven by hatred. Although we are often deceived by the world and the devil, it is the flesh that fools us the most. We make the demonic the significant force when, in reality, it is the flesh. Far more comes from the weakness of the flesh than from the devil. We give him credit and blame him for too much.

We don't hear God's whisper because we listen to our own voices, which speak too loudly. When people whisper, we think that they are also deaf, so we shout. Our knowledge drowns out divine reality because we believe in the trap of repetition of life's situations. We are caught in the rut of failure. And although God promises we will be overcomers, our experience speaks too loudly.

That is what God says. But it is not what we believe. Our repeated breakdown in the face of temptation seems to contradict that promise. It is because we are standing on the fringes. We don't really know God; therefore, we do not trust him fully. We fail to hear because we don't think there is anything else to hear. We have a level of spiritual understanding that accumulates with time. But all this perception is but the faint whisper of God. 'For we know in part and we prophesy in part. But when that which is perfect has come, then that which is in part will be done away.'[299] Eventually, the 'part' becomes the whole, as we stop growing in God's revelation. Contentedness surpasses the vital need for the pursuit of God. We acquire other channels of satisfaction. We allow ourselves to be diverted by the normal and everyday improvements of living and the spiralling upward success of life that accompanies its diligent pursuit.

We forget that God is coming, and we become contented with the now – the part, not the future perfection. There is nothing wrong with enjoying the immediate and sampling the success of conscientiousness, but often this promotion silences God. He sounds a warning, but we don't know where it is coming from. We fail to hear because we are facing in the wrong direction. When God speaks, he usually speaks clearly. But we are often confused because we don't seem to know which direction the divine sound is coming from.

In 1986, I was invited as the only UK minister to Impetus '86, an international conference in Sri Lanka, where 800 delegates from sixty-three nations were gathering. The subject they chose for me was 'worship'. Canon Derek Hong from Singapore did the leadership of worship, and I did congregational response; the two overlapped. When I arrived at the conference three hours late because of plane connections, I was greeted by the chairman, who said, 'We have distributed your advance paper on worship to all those attending, and now we wish you to speak on "Into the Presence".' I was nonplussed, for I had only prepared to speak once at the conference and once at the Sunday morning service, where I was to lead the 5,000-strong church plus delegates in Colombo. I had never spoken on 'Into the Presence', so I went to my hotel room that night and sought God for revelation. Thankfully, He gave me twenty points for the next morning.

After I had preached, I was thronged and beseeched by people from all over the world to go to their country and speak the same. I thanked them for their kind invitations but sadly declined because of my wife's condition back in London; she was my first pledge in life. Because I honoured that vow, when I started HICC with my wife, at the first meeting in my house, we had six people, each from a different country. The multinational church had begun. Because I couldn't go to them, God sent the world to me. He took two years to start that process. He saw Patricia's sickness, her faith, and my loyalty and put things in motion. Never underestimate God. He has ways and means to bring His will to pass.

The edges conceal the full authority and almightiness of God. Wherever Jesus went, he caused confusion and apoplexy among religious people.

He didn't do things that normal people did. We think we know and can anticipate, but not Jesus. He turned water into wine, spat on mud and wiped it onto eyes, walked on water, fed 5,000 with a few sardines and biscuits, and kept his income tax in a fish's mouth. We think we know Jesus, but suddenly we realise we don't. He surprises us all along the way. The edges seem to explain God, but then he moves differently from what we anticipated. Throughout history, he did things differently. And as we read and experience His wonderful blessing and answers to prayer personally, we perceive that we didn't know God at all.

Just cast your mind over God's way with money – that's always bordering on the edges of understanding. The world has a saying: 'Get all you can, can all you get and then guard the can.'[300] The system of the world hoards and banks its wealth, and inflation robs it of its value. The entire economic order of society is crumbling. The entire argument between the major political parties is over the acquisition and distribution of wealth. The world's system is motivated and sponsored by the devil who wanted to steal God's throne and has worked into humanity a stingy 'grabbingnness' a self-possessing covetousness. But the Godly way is different: 'There is one who scatters, yet increases more; and there is one who withholds more than is right, but it leads to poverty. The generous soul will be made rich, and he who waters will also be watered himself.'[301]

We think we know what love is until we meet God, and even then, we but touch the edges, or the shoreline. When Lazarus was sick unto death, Jesus delayed his coming. The two sisters were distraught and blamed Jesus. But at the edges of His revelation, He was explaining and revealing the reality of resurrection – not belief *in* resurrection but resurrection faith. The weeping woman at his feet showed beyond the edges of God. Jeus said: "she has anointed me for burial"[302] perhaps unwhttingly, but certainly prophetically. Religion curled its toes and rejected her emotional outburst. Jesus accepted it as normal and encouraged it. He loved sinners, and his passion was for their life. Her action brought into focus the pain of his suffering and the pleasure of his love. But even then it only shows the edges of his love. When you look down on the edge of a knife, any light will reflect off a blunt blade. When you look down on God, there is no light reflected. He is so sharp we can't see past the edges, but common sense tells us that there must be more than the edge.

Jesus touched people when he could but speak the word of healing. 'He touched her hand and the fever left her.'[303] There are three ways we can communicate – we can speak, we can articulate through art, and lastly we can touch or show action. The first two may fail, but the last one can remedy difficult situations. When the prodigal son returned, the father fell on his neck and kissed him. Jesus touched the grubby hands of children and, in that action, wrote volumes on how to deal with children. Although Jesus gave deathless words of hope, probably his greatest service was to touch a leper.

His touch, to Peter's mother-in-law, kindled great expectancy. It strengthens a patient's faith. We often need that, and weekly, we look for his touch because we repeat our tendency to sin and lose battles. Alexander Pope said, 'Blessed are those who expect nothing for they will not be disappointed.' Years on, we still have the same humiliating temptations that plague us; and we need His touch. We have constant weaknesses that ever disable us; we need His touch. He wants to reverse our tendency to lose faith and to cry out, 'Blessed are they who expect everything, who expect the impossible, who look past the edges, who see the impossible happen by faith.'

This story reveals that God never distances Himself from our sins and sicknesses. Many will, but not He. With MSR about in hospitals, we are cautious about contagion, but that is never God's way of dealing with life. God is not fastidious. Bethlehem was just that – God touching man by taking human form. When God came in the form of Jesus, He touched us; He didn't stand aloof. He showed us the fringes or the edges in Jesus. But there is much more. Will He not with Him give us all things? The Pharisees stood aloof and condemned from their own standard of holiness, throwing a copper to a pauper, their conscience settled, and then paraded their generosity in the temple. But Jesus mingled with and touched the paupers.

He transcends time and, therefore, eternity. He lingers in eternity. And, therefore, we miss the background, being too occupied with the foreground. 'We look not at the things which are seen, but at the things which are not seen: for the things that are seen are temporal; but the things which are not seen are eternal.'[304] As if carrying two shopping bags, one in either hand, God travels through time being able to dip into either the past or future. We look at the fierce economic pressures, the political uncertainty, the violence and vandalism, and the international conflicts, all suggesting potential catastrophes. Because we are listening to the fury of disorder and treading in the fringes of knowledge, we cannot see the answer to all this global and personal unrest. We inhabit two worlds and have forgotten the conflicts that rage between the two.

Inhabiting two eternities does not mean the two are in direct opposition to each other; it simply means we are restricted in our understanding of the divine plan for both. We see the truth but not the whole truth. We see the small details, not the whole picture. We, as a church, are to explain the foreground in the light of the background. We are to attempt to open eyes to the chariots of the Lord hidden in the invisible realm of defence. This aids us in our understanding of personal trials and opposition – knowing that, behind the scenes, God is at work.

Chapter 15

Shattered Dreams

For you have need of endurance, so that when you have done
the will of God, you may receive what was promised.
—Hebrews 10:36

The secret of God's dream, and we should be very careful to prove he did give it, is that it will eventually 'come to pass'. But we often forget that 'obstacles are those frightful things you see when you take your eyes off your goals.' God is an expert at delays, for while we wait, we mature so that we are can handle the reward. If the fulfilment is too early, it could kill us off. Unfortunately, too often, our lives often correspond to our convictions. It is a question of *our whims* or *His will*. His will took Jacob to Haran for twenty years, Moses to the backside of the desert for forty years. And Jesus had to wait eighteen years before he could start his ministry. The dark seasons of the soul have more to do with our inability to focus on God's timing than on actual inability to perform.

We bow to idols in our minds due to lies of the devil. The biggest idol is the one called failure. We believe we were wrong in accepting the call or dreaming the dream. Or perhaps God got it wrong! Failure is failing to fulfil God's will, and he never gives a dream that is impossible to fulfil. There are many words for a dream – ambition, achievement, goal, objective, or vision, to name a few. All add up to a driving force; like glue in our lungs, we cannot get rid of it. It is also usually within our limitations. 'If you would hit the mark, you must aim a little above it; every arrow it flies feels the attraction of earth.'[305] The stretch for God is normal, and long arms go together in the kingdom.

If you never had a dream, perhaps God never intended you to have one. His desire might be that you are just ordinary, *but being good at being ordinary is a special task.* There are 62 million people in Britain, but only eleven are in the world cup; those footballers who are not are not failures. They are just ordinary. And those special eleven would have nobody to play against if all the others sulked! Paul said, 'I have learned to be content' – he was content with who he was and where he was; perhaps that was God's will also! This attitude does not negate the dream, but it might interpret it.

Shattered dreams

However, most Christians have dreams in God, dreams that take them on an exciting adventure to expected fulfilment. But sometimes that anticipated goal is never reached, and the delay is such that hope fails. 'Hope deferred makes the heart sick.'[306] And we are, at times, very sick because we are very disappointed. God speaks to us in the midst of life, and we respond to his calling. We commence with high hopes and a fervent spirit as the door of opportunity swings wide. Soon problems ensue, and opposition arises. The adversary of our soul makes things quite plain – we're failures; our dreams will never come to fruition. We believe his lies and both dismay and depression stalk our heels as we begin to doubt God and His will for us.

We are sure we heard correctly when we saw the dream with an eye of faith. Our conviction was based on hearing and knowing God's voice. So why is that we are now fumbling to find adequate words to explain the uncertainty and sense of worthlessness we feel? Did God make a mistake? If He did, why? And if not, did we misread His will for us? Questions race through our troubled mind as we compare scripture against the prophetic word. We find we are destined for glory but live in the dust and ashes of a burnt-out hope. We feel flat and lifeless as we struggle to testify of God's grace. Our self-esteem is dented, and we are embarrassed. That kind of scenario is not new; it has dogged the footsteps of many saints for countless generations. I write this to you today in an attempt to reinforce your hope in God and to provide pillars or underpinning support when your world is crumbling.

To clarify the word *deferred* in our text – '*hope deferred*' – we need to explain it better. It also means to 'elongate or to extend'. As you reach for your destiny, it stretches ahead of you, and you never quite catch up with it. Months grow into years, and you seem no nearer your destiny. It is so extended that you can never grasp it' it outreaches your stretch.

Naomi, in the Old Testament, went down to Moab at the height of the Bethlehem famine, but her husband and two sons died in that adopted country. Her dream of sufficiency became a nightmare as she buried all her family except her two daughters-in-law. Ten years later, it was at last fulfilled because God wanted the best for her, not the worst. 'The thief does not come except to steal, and to kill.'[307] And his one overruling aim is to subvert our trust in God.

Our problem is time and interpretation. We are impatient for the dream to be fulfilled and often ignorant of what God really wants. The book of Revelation is such a case, for hardly anyone gets the interpretation correct. We are often mistaken, for we think God needs to work on our timescale. We frequently misread the language of the Spirit, because we try to decipher spiritual things with natural understanding.

Earth movers

The people who make things happen are dreamers. It was T. E. Lawrence who said, 'All men dream: but not equally. Those who dream by night in the dusty recesses of their minds wake in the day to find that it was vanity: but the dreamers of the day are dangerous men, for they may act their dream with open eyes, to make it possible.'

Martin Luther King was such a man. So powerful was his dream that he was assassinated. This is a quote from one of his most famous speeches: 'I have a dream that one day this nation will rise up, live out the true meaning of its creed: we hold these truths to be self-evident, that all men are created equal.'[308]

All of us need anchors to hold our souls steady in the turbulence of life. Dreams are those weights that stabilise us against the currents of public opinion and opposition. They drag on the seabed of impossibility, thus giving us confidence amid the raging storms around us. Daydreamers usually succeed with God. God had a dream, and Jesus was the answer. 'He shall see the labour of His soul, and be satisfied. By His knowledge My righteous Servant shall justify many, for He shall bear their iniquities.'[309] That was God's purpose, goal, dream or vision – for Jesus to bear the sin of the whole world. It was accomplished. Nothing deterred Him, yet all hell tried to subvert that cause.

Confirm the accuracy of the promise to you. Dreams that count are engineered and manufactured by the Spirit. It is not our wild schemes that God will bless but his designated gift. 'I press toward the goal for the prize of the upward call of God in Christ Jesus.'[310] The upward call should be the centre of our dream. There will be the competitive call from beneath that is challenged by the upward pull of God's Spirit. God-given dreams have a touch of unreality, yet they lie within the compass of possibility. Neither could a dumb man be a preacher nor a blind man a guide, so be realistic.

Keep one non-negotiable option open

We are our own biggest deterrents to fulfilling our dreams. We can talk ourselves into or out of anything we want. It depends on what we want. Be diligent. 'Do not become sluggish, but imitate those who through faith and patience inherit the promises.'[311] Sluggish means (literally) lazy or (figuratively) stupid, dull, or slothful. Often, we give up too easily because the way gets tough.

Keep one non-negotiable option open – pursue your dream single-mindedly. Many will be the setbacks, many the obstacles, but single-mindedness will win through. The dark seasons of the soul are more to do with our inability to focus on God's timing than with actual inability to perform. When the going gets tough, lash yourself to the mast – you aren't going to be swept overboard. The boat may sink, but you're not going down with it. It is that firm mental attitude that refuses to give in, even in the most violent of storms.

The world does not care one hoot about our difficulties; it cares whether we can cross the finishing line. We are not here to whine and whimper but to make good decisions that ensure we finish the race. Nobody wants to know your problems. They want to know how you won. Starting is relatively easily compared to the long haul of finishing.

Ensure you are not too comfortable

Rid yourself of the protectionism that comes from the blight of security. A good religion with a heavenly father – good politics with a protective government – a good society with a plethora of philanthropists will stifle dreams. Most Christian parents spoil their children, for they over-provide. Children must be challenged to find their potential. The church is a place where creative genius can succeed; the only thing preventing success is *you*.

When conditions are too favourable, sloth enters, and people rest on their laurels. Israel wanted to return to Egypt with the onions and garlic – it was comfortable under bondage, challenging in the wilderness. A Russian Jew was sent home to Israel. He was given a barbers shop by the state but complained that they didn't provide him with customers. The communist state had sapped his initiative. Dreams fade when our situation improves because dreams often depend on us striving to fulfil them. Nothing is given easily; it would not be appreciated.

Contrary circumstances do not mean a withdrawal of the promise or calling. We are wrestling at this end of time with the spirit of lawlessness. The love of many diminishes, and rebellion abounds. Satan is loose and waging unremitting war on the saints. Some of the adversity we experience is due to the direct confrontation of hell's anger. 'And because lawlessness will abound, the love of many will grow cold.'[312] Take heart from the encouragement of the apostle who withstood the wild beasts at Ephesus: 'Therefore, my beloved brethren, be steadfast, immovable, always abounding in the work of the Lord, knowing that your labor is not in vain in the Lord.'[313]

The underworld often goes unnoticed

We tend to underestimate the underworld. Our induced blindness to interference from another world is undergirded by an intellectualism that disbands theories about the Prince of Darkness and rests on a more humanistic approach to apparent failure. Because we don't see the works of darkness as readily evident – the spirit of the world laughs at such things – we tend towards identifying ourselves with that viewpoint and look to our limitations, rather than accept that we are being attacked at our root belief in God.

God has promised his care and love for us and that he will never abandon us. Yet we struggle to see his hand in contrary currents, secretly blaming ourselves because, if God is good, then this turnabout in fortune must be because we have done something wrong. Remember that the devil wants the worst for you, and God wants His best for you. Often our struggles are not with the weakness of the flesh but with the hordes of hell. He is out to make you believe his lies. And if he can do that, he has a hold over you that will thwart the God-given dreams of destiny. Exercise faith and reject the devil. Believe in yourself and God and despise the devil's tricks and temptations. 'Now the just shall live by faith; but if anyone draws back, my soul has no pleasure in him.'[314]

Patiently Do (2 Samuel 1:17–18)

When we face disappointment, sorrow, despair, and outright opposition that leaves us bewildered, hurt, in pain, and hopeless, then this text will help us. We all need a pull upwards into action at some time in our lives, an applied force that will redirect us to focus when sorrow turns our noonday into midnight.

Saul and Jonathan were dead, killed by Philistine forces, in particular felled by their archers. As David was sorrowing and lamenting (wailing) in his pain, he spoke a word of wisdom that echoes to us all. 'And David lamented with this lamentation over Saul and over Jonathan his son: Also he bade them teach the children of Judah the use of the bow.'[315]

David's sorrow manifested itself in a regime of remedial action. Out of that lament arose a need to redirect the attention of the people of Judah. The king and the crown were dead, and David wrote a song that the daughters of Israel might sing. But beyond that exigency, there was a need to purge their sorrow in constructive labour.

We all face sorrow at some time, and the tendency is to shut oneself away and linger on what might have been. Out of that negative attitude, there can emerge a critical spirit against God. David, when he sinned with Bathsheba, was faced with a dilemma. And as the resultant child lay sick unto death, he prayed upon the matter. He said this: 'But now he is dead, wherefore should I fast? Can I bring him back again? I shall go to him, but he shall not return to me.'[316] In other words, if the situation cannot be changed, life must go on.

Rather than contemplate sadness and misery, *set out to cut out* some new destiny. Become industrious in the things of the kingdom. Work is the healthiest thing in this world; it is the highest form of therapy. Perhaps you may have undertaken some project for God, and it seems to have failed. If it has, then throw yourself into something akin to it and employ your time. Get away from the known and humdrum and do something special that excites you.

From personal experience, I know that work is the best therapy in crisis. To bury oneself in one's work is better than being prematurely buried through worry, for worry is mental theft. We all need distractions to help us cope with heart-rending ghettos of emotional deprivation. There are practical means of solving problems, and you do not have to be a spiritual superman. Plain common sense is all it takes.

Personally speaking, I did five jobs to help in the midst of suffering. I took a higher degree, worked as a subject tutor for three degrees, was the associate minister of a church, rebuilt a bungalow, pioneered and developed my own private business, and looked after my wife Patricia in her illness. Keeping five balls in the air was no mean feat, but it helped keep my thoughts on God and not on worry about Patricia's disease. If I had sat still and moped, it would have finished me. But instead, I was able to rise up and get on with life.

When Jesus died and rose again, the disciples were forlorn because their Saviour, friend, and intended king had apparently gone. However, Jesus appeared to them after the resurrection and asked the disciples to meet him in Galilee. They went to the seashore, and Jesus was not there. So Peter said, 'I go a fishing.'[317] It was his release valve; good for him! He was, no doubt, disillusioned and probably thought that Christ would not appear. He, therefore, returned to his previous occupation in disappointment. Doing so would take the strain out of waiting. He was a wise man. People have criticised him for this action, but then they were never in that situation. Rather than sitting moaning in the sand, he took advantage of the environment and set about rowing. He didn't catch anything, but at least, his mind was occupied with not catching anything.

Sitting still is no answer to life. God made us for occupation. Scientists have found that there is a bacteria in the soil that helps ward off depression, and God made Adam a gardener. Getting your hands dirty is excellent medicine. Gardeners are usually sane and sensible, unhurried and calm. However, if you do have to sit still in complete inertia, endeavour to wait *on* God as you wait *in* Him and *for* Him. For in Him, 'we move and have our being'.[318] And those who wait on the Lord will rise up, walk, run, and not be weary.[319] They *shall* overcome. What does the Word say? 'By your patience possess your souls.' [320]

'You need to keep on patiently doing God's will if you want him to do for you all that he has promised.'[321] Our dreams to be valid must be linked to God's promises. Otherwise, they are human fantasies. Joseph's dreams were based on God's call and commission. So were Jacob's.[322] God must be in the place of the dream. 'Then Jacob awoke from his sleep and said, "Surely the LORD is in this place, and I did not know it."'[323] Some dreams are midnight indigestion and certainly not sponsored by God. But there are times in our life when unmistakably God speaks, and we know without any doubt that he has called us to destiny. Times and people may become difficult, but knowing that He has pledged himself for us, we plough on. George Bush said this: 'It's not whether people like you but whether they share the bright dreams…and understand the heartbeat of the country.'[324]

People's cooperation can be harnessed if they know that you stand for something that has a divine stamp and origin about it. God can demolish mountains of opposition planted as obstacles to impair our way and counter the violent attack on our vision. Joseph is such a case. 'And they [his brothers] said one to another, Behold, this dreamer comes. Come now therefore, and let us slay him, and cast him into some pit, and we will say, some evil beast has devoured him: and we shall see what will become of his dreams.'[325] Thirteen years later, his dream was fulfilled. God turned the evil into victory. Psalm 105 confirms this.

Never try and interpret your dreams based on human reason. In France around 1919, surrealism, a movement in art and literature, began. It sought to resolve the contradictory conditions of *dream* and *reality* into an absolute reality by various techniques, thus escaping the dominance of reason and conscious control. The result was visual chaos that defied understanding. The same will happen in our lives if we attempt to apply human reasoning to God's will. Often, our reasoning and God's plan seem completely contradictory. Thus, the result will appear to be complete chaos. It's best not to try and interpret God's will; rather, leave it to God. We will always put two heads on things if we attempt this faulty interpretation of situations.

Cast down vile imaginations

Remember this if you remember nothing else. God does not repent in His choosing. His gifts are sure and steadfast, as is His calling. He did not make a mistake when He chose us. 'For the gifts and the calling of God are irrevocable.'[326] The devil will whisper that God made a mistake when he chose you, but it's a lie from the 'Father of lies'. Paul says this, and he spoke from experience, being often hassled by the underworld: 'Being confident of this very thing, that He who has begun a good work in you will complete it until the day of Jesus Christ.'[327] And he also said, 'For it is God who works in you both to will and to do for His good pleasure.'[328]

We are warriors, not whimperers, battle-scarred veterans of a long-lasting war. God has unfurled His ensign over us. God is love – and that means he will provide all of heaven's resources to assist in our campaign. God leads us in triumph, and consternation arises because, in fighting an invisible foe, we don't see the result of our victory. Therefore, we think we are failures.[329]

Our greatest test is discouragement, and the devil is a master strategist when it comes to developing ways of corrupting our confidence. We may resist temptation and walk in righteousness, refusing to succumb to the allurement of compromise, yet fall foul of his wily schemes and, thus, reap despair. If he can make us fretful, he has won round one. We begin to rest on our worry and not the finished work of Christ. While we fret about productivity and success, the Bible clearly states the obvious: 'So then neither he who plants is anything, nor he who waters, but God who gives the increase.'[330] Tucked away in Psalm 104:14, we read this comforting word: 'He causes the grass to grow for the cattle, and vegetation for the service of man, that he may bring forth food from the earth.' Let this promise encourage us. He who spans the heavens has time to see that a humble cow is fed. Are we not much more valuable than cattle?

And if so, we can reliably rest on His love to oversee our condition and calling.

It is not a question of sterile confidence that leaves all to Him and abandons ministry in a Calvinistic way of life. Rather, it's about waiting on His good pleasure to bring to pass His will in our lives with a purpose that glorifies Him. This is where the Cross comes in. We have to completely surrender our own feelings, schemes, plans, and motivations. It's not important how we look in the eyes of other people. What matters is whether our commendation[331] comes from God. Are we in the right place, at the right time, in the right attitude? If so, leave it to Him.

The devil will not only work discouragement, he'll also cause confusion. The Cross was apparent confusion; the disciples were aghast at the result of Christ's life. It seemed a tragedy and a final exit of failure; the expected kingdom – misinterpreted – seemed an impossibility. At first sight, it appeared that the hordes of darkness had triumphed. In the eyes of Christ's followers, the teachings of Jesus were buried in a cave grave, wrapped as he was for burial. Confusion indeed!

Then came Sunday. Sundays always come. Fridays frighten us. Sundays always will come, but in three days. And that's the problem – the three days of Calvary. Then will come the victory; then will come the triumph. The Cross teaches us that the final triumph is always in Christ's hands.

We are told that we are 'more than conquerors', and that means we win without fighting, for the battle is the Lord's, and we simply stand and wait for his glory to enact demolition on our enemies. In the film *Bridge of Spies*, James Donovan (played by Tom Hanks), at the request of the American government negotiates the prisoner exchange of Gary Powers, an American spy plane pilot, for a captured Russian spy named Rudolf Abel. Rudolf, whilst speaking to Donovan, tells him of a family member who looked a most unlikely candidate for heroics, who rarely spoke and was almost invisible. But one day, the home was invaded by the secret police, who beat him. And afterwards, he got up, so they beat him again. He got up again, so they beat him a third time. And still he got up, so they left him alone. He was called from that day 'the standing man'. Trial and adversity come into our homes and beat us, apparently unmercifully, and we are knocked down. But we had better stand up again in Christ. 'For greater is he that is in us than he that is in the world.'[332]

Chapter 16

Red Markers

"For we do not commend ourselves again to you, but give you opportunity to glory on our behalf, that you may have an answer for those who boast in appearance and not in heart."
—2 Corinthians 5:12

Elizabeth Mortimer won the Military Medal for exceptional courage during the Luftwaffe's sustained assault on Biggin Hill, Kent, the celebrated sector station for RAF Fighter Command in the Battle of Britain. The airfield was pockmarked with craters and littered with unexploded bombs.

On Sunday, 18 August 1940, she ran onto the airfield with red marker flags to pinpoint these unexploded bombs so that the incoming Spitfire and Hurricane pilots returning from combat could land safely. Although commanded to stop by an officer, she continued after his back was turned.[333] Such courage was duly rewarded, but what of those unnoticed Christians who constantly put themselves under satanic attack as they located the minefields of temptation exposing to those who are in active conflict the perils of the landing site?

God wants to establish red flag markers so that those who follow have some guidelines to prevent accidents and disaster for coming generations. David expressed this same wish: 'And now that I am old and grey, don't forsake me. Give me time to tell this new generation (and their children too) about all your mighty miracles.'[334]

The three young men in Daniel 3 illustrate for us an attitude and conviction to service that warns all who tread a similar pathway about the refiner's fire. Shadrach, Meshach, and Abednego, without thought for themselves, endangered their lives so that those, who profess faith in God, and who would follow in the future, would, like modern war planes, be able to land amidst dangerous conditions. Hear their reply: 'But if he doesn't, please understand, sir, that even then we will never under any circumstance serve your gods or worship the gold statue you have erected.'[335] These men demonstrated not only faith but also courage. With faith, they made a decisive choice based on previous irrefutable experience – God is for us.

Dangerous lifestyle

God calls us to a dangerous lifestyle. Being a Christian is not the life of a sissy. All who profess His name will live through hazardous experiences that are the guarantee of discipleship. I would be less than honest if I didn't warn you that there could come a time when the fire is heated seven times hotter. The three young Hebrew men illustrated to us the inevitable challenge of service. The story maps out large pinnacles of faith, faith that carried them through.

Paul's hope for New Testament Christians is that they have an answer to those who boast in an outward manifestation of works but not an inward condition of spiritual reality. Above all things, God wants our *internal life* to be as whole as the outside *appears*. If our private is not our public He may make our private public. His love could not let Him desire otherwise, for what lasts must last in eternity, where real value is assessed.

Red flag markers

There are critical circumstances that seem to circumvent our natural flow of destiny. Thus we all wish for a settled and contented life, free from harsh realities that burn into us lasting lessons from trial. But, sometimes these adversities act like a built wall to hem or shut us in and imprison us in a way that seems to thawart God's divine plan for our life. In my own experience, my first wife's sickness prevented me from doing many things which I would have liked to have done, that seemd, in my opnion, to thwart God's plans for my life. However, the compensation was a knowledge of the Bible that was fundmental to the preaching and ministering stance, gained though many midnight hours alone with God on my knees in my study, resisting the dull ache of enforced celibacy. Hemmed in indeed. The blessing was that each congregation I spoke to were taught and grew both spiritually and numerically, especially in London. What I did in private God rewarded openly.

Faith is the language that surmounts the critical circumstances that often seem to circumvent our walk towards destiny. Shadrach, Meshach, and Abednego had their future rudely interrupted. Yet they remained loyal to their God. And even when the furnace threatened them, they did not bend. They were people in charge of Babylonian affairs, not just secular workers. They were top men, and they faced certain death. Their hats indicated their rank. Their rank did not save them, but God did. Our position in life does not exempt us from the fire. Sometimes, as promotions increase, so do the fires.

In *His* hands!

The scriptures and our own lives are replete with instances that upset our well-laid plans, which we sometimes mistakenly interpret as God's plans. Often, His thoughts are not our thoughts, and His ways will, at times, confound our sensibilities and understanding. God does not explain Himself or apologise, for in our commitment to His forgiveness, we were bought with a price; He is sovereign of our future.

David was to be king – Samuel anointed him to that future – but he was chased like a partridge on the mountains by the wild and jealous Saul, who openly declared his intent to kill him. That was part of his destiny. God kept him until the wheel turned full circle. 'There's a divinity that shapes our ends, rough-hew them how we will.'[336] God will make it work; He was a carpenter, and carpenters always make things work!

Our adherence to principles attracts unwelcome persecution. It was Spurgeon who said, 'When you see no present advantage, then walk by faith and not by sight.'[337] Those who adhere to principle will suffer loss, but not real loss. For if we 'seek first the kingdom of God and His righteousness...all these things shall be added to you [us].'[338] God does not leave debts he will repay because 'godliness...is great gain'.[339] The promise of God is that he is 'a sun and shield, the LORD will give grace and glory; no good thing will He withhold from those who walk uprightly.'[340] The furnace in Nebuchadnezzar's day was a 'good thing', for it taught these young men to apply faith to a specific situation. Those who walk in righteousness will attract persecution and ridicule. We should never expect exemption from the discomfort of opposition, for if we set a standard, there will always be those who try to defy and malign it.

God turns general principles into particular deliverances. When Jesus walked back into the lives of Mary and Martha, having delayed for four days, he was out to prove to them that, although he was the ultimate 'resurrection and the life', he was also a *present* resurrection and life. They were looking down an anticipated future history to *the* great resurrection day; he was teaching them that His power was currently available. They were removing the power of resurrection from their particular situation. It was, to them, a future end-time mentality, which often pervades the contemporary church. Jesus was adjusting their focus, to turn end speculations into *now* realities.

When you can feel the heat of the flames, there is a tendency to look to the grave, believing that, in the end, all will be well. But in doing that, we forget that God can work now, defying natural laws. He is not subject to earthly terror, because He is above nature. He was reigning before the world was created.

The discriminating power of God's fire breaks bonds. All the three young men lost in the furnace were their bonds. The advantage of a furnace is that God turns things on their head; often, a bird sings sweeter when in a cage. God uses iron bars and bitumen fires to break our shackles. God breaks those bonds that are too foundational in our lives. He is our foundation, not our feelings and emotions. All of us are too enamoured with earth, and even as the eaglet is pushed from the nest, so God can do likewise with us and, He can also shake the tree.

The ultimate victory

The important principal point is that God did not deliver Shadrach, Meshach, and Abednego *from* this furnace; he delivered them *in* it. There is a modern misconception that defeats many Christians before they start to walk the pilgrim way. They believe that ultimate victory is to be released from the flames and the heat of the furnace, but it isn't. Ultimate victory is to reach maturity, and that is not age related, it is spiritual perception and action. God wants our transformation and to lift our faith so we can trust Him implicitly in whatever circumstance prevails.

God didn't answer the prayer of these three young men. They must have prayed – fervently! By *not* answering them, God helped them find a new dimension of faith and a new level of grace. God wants to ensure that our faith is 'fire-proof',[341] and to do that, He often does not explain Himself. We do not read of others being cast into a furnace, and there is no reason we should. This was their trial, not ours. Dross is not thrown into the fire; it has no value, only gold and silver. *If you're in the fire, you must be worth it.*

Jesus walks with those who abandon themselves to His higher destiny. Fires will come in many ways. Man's harshness to people is but one of them. History is packed with examples of evil wrought upon those who profess Jesus as Saviour.[342] One fire that burns in this twentieth century is *oppression*, oppression similar to that which gripped the children of Israel in Egypt. This kind of oppression scorches life to the core. Numerous regimes across this globe are branded persecutors, treading down countless believers without pity or respite. It continues today, and there are those who, whatever the circumstance, will tread upon the image of God in man. The intervention by Amnesty International is a constant reminder of the continuing inequity against humankind, which is often worse than any other calamity.

Who has not experienced the vicious flame of *slander*, whose hurt smoulders in the soul as people bring false witness against us? We are helpless to defend ourselves, as the slanderers run rampant over our testimony with lies and mendacity. 'Vengeance is mine,' says the Lord, but we wish we could wield a sword and bring our own form of justice. And not defending ourselves is a constant source of frustration, as we submit to His authority and leave it alone. He will eventually repay, but our impatience rankles in our spirit.

By far the greatest fire is that which Satan brings upon us; there is *temptation* that dogs our footsteps, as it did Jesus in the wilderness. He excuses no one and knows our weakest link. 'But as for me, I came so close to the edge of the cliff! My feet were slipping and I was almost gone."[343] All too often, the psalmist echoes our sentiments as we struggle against raging trials fashioned by the prince of the air, that subtle adversary of our soul. As we strive to overcome his conspiracy, he plants a sting in our conscience, the thought of failing our Lord. He never leaves us alone, even as Jesus promises never to forsake us. That is why we have the victory.

There are those who walk alone now and will do so in eternity

We read that a fourth man appeared in the fire like unto the Son of God. The three young men of Daniel would not have had this glorious revelation and companionship if they had not been in the fire. The recompense of faith is that Jesus comes with us.[344] Look also in the Minor Prophets: 'I will bring the third that remain through the fire and make them pure, as gold and silver are refined and purified by fire.'[345] The word to us is that 'through much tribulation we inherit the kingdom.'[346] In that tribulation, we will have a constant companion, who will never leave us or forsake us. He will be with us until His perfect will has been done. We will never know Jesus fully until we have felt Calvary. The servant will not be above his master.

A pigeon fancier clipped the wings of a bird he sold and it *walked* sixty miles back home. It defies understanding that a bird could do that, but without the fire of those situations, that bird would never have accomplished such an amazing feat! God puts us in the fire or clips our wings so that we can walk – with Jesus. The women with alabaster box of ointment broke the flask to release the perfume, the gapes from the vineyard need to be crushed to obtain the wine, and rose petals are crushed for the fragrance. That's the spiritual life. Fire and water can be either good or bad; it depends on circumstances. God orders the circumstances.

But what of those who have not made God their trust? Death is not annihilation but a fire that burns without end. Jesus will not tread that fire, for He only walks with those who put their faith in Him. He did go to hell. He is not going again. He went there and back for us so that we do not have to go there.

Chapter 17

Limping into Blessing (Genesis 25–35)

Writer Olga Craig reported this in the *Sunday Telegraph*:

Darting between the overhanging cliffs, a boy scrambles over razor-sharp rocks and then reaches out for a helping hand to pull him up. Crouched in the entrance to the cave 14-year-old Kalin grabs the bedraggled youngster and hauls him into the freezing cavern. Scrambling on hands and knees they push aside the clutter of dirty clothes, rotting food, empty milk cartons and plastic bags and settle down on the cave floor carpeted with stinking layers of horse chestnut leaves. Amid the squalor of the cave on the outskirts of Cluj in western Romania, it is time for supper.

Kicking off his torn moon boots and, wrapping the frayed and stained jacket of an outsized man's suit around his skinny frame, Kalin snatches at the mound of stale vegetables stolen from the town's market and munches hungrily. At his feet is a tub of industrial

glue that will provide desert - sniffed from one of the
plastic bags strewn at his feet.[347]

In this excerpt, two boys in gross conditions find help in each other's touch. We count the conditions described here as horrendous. But to the boys, this is a moment of fellowship in the privation and pain of life.

There is an Indian caste called 'the untouchable', or Harijan. They are members of the lowest Indian caste, formerly forbidden to be touched by members of the other castes. How sad to be excluded from a common touch. Jesus identified with humankind in our hurts, fallibility, and pain. It is said of him: 'For we have not an high priest which cannot be touched with the feeling of our infirmities; but was in all points tempted like as we are, yet without sin.'[348] Because He can be touched, He can touch. God touches humanity and heals people. People touch people and often injure them.

When my wife was in an intensive care unit and on a ventilator, paralysed because her drugs had been withdrawn, all I could do was stroke her head. Words meant very little at a time like that. There are some situations where a touch can mean more than a thousand words. A car is wrecked on a highway, and through the mangled wreckage, someone struggles to reach the imprisoned victim and is just able to touch his or her fingers. Words don't matter; it is a human response to a desperate need.

Jesus came with a new order for children and suffered them to come to him. He took them up in his arms and touched them. The disciples tried to prevent him, but he knew that children need the touch of love; it builds security and confidence. Over and above all the great sermons Jesus must have preached, the most graphic was when he reached down and touched the leper – this demonstrated agape love. He spoke great words like these: 'And the King shall answer and say unto them, verily I say unto you, Inasmuch as ye have done it unto one of the least of these my brethren, ye have done it unto me.'[349] Great though His words were, He did more by taking the children in his arms than through all the eloquent sermons in His lifetime. How would you like to be touched by God?

The touch of Jesus creates an expectation of divine disclosure. He did it to quicken faith, strengthen hope, and put people at the door of reception. Anyone receiving his touch would expect something to happen. Expectation goes a long way to solving the problem. James says this: 'You have not because you ask not.'[350] We don't ask because we don't expect. 'Blessed are those who expect nothing for they shall not be disappointed.'[351]

At some point, his hand touches us in that inward pain, struggle, and passion. He touches us by one million things and in a million ways – a tear, the glimpse of a friend, a soft word of encouragement, a hymn, a specific scripture, or a sermon. God is not stumped for methods of communication; he can devise a plan and fulfil it.

There is not only the expectation of divine disclosure and impartation but the establishment of godly truth – the truth that God never distances Himself from our needs. He does not operate from a safe distance. Bethlehem proves it. He came down to our level; God in Christ touched us. God came. In the Old Testament, they devised a regime whereby the unclean were excluded, and no one ever touched them; these 'untouchables' were kept outside the camp. When Jesus came, He reversed all that. 'Wherefore Jesus also, that he might sanctify the people with his own blood, suffered without the gate.'[352] The religious leaders threw help like coppers from a distance so they wouldn't be contaminated. Not Jesus, not then, not now. He touched a woman, and the fever left her.[353] He can touch our fever of anxiety through the days of suffering and pain.

Achieving ambition

When Jesus touches us through the Spirit, He often deposits a vision, which produces a desire for success or a strong feeling of wanting to achieve great things. It is sometimes an undue craving for honour or striving for popular favour, for dreaming is inextricably linked to ambition. Countless people have made a success of their lives, and many today are in popular and visible evidence of that desire. But also many have failed and have a misplaced desire for glory. In the church corporate, this situation is often the cause of great disappointment and a sensation of being unfulfilled, which gives rise to anxious worry and frustration.

Jonny Depp said, 'For me, ambition has become a dirty word. I prefer hunger.' And The Buddha said, 'Ambition is like love, impatient both of delays and rivals.' In the words of British poet, Robert Browning, "Ah, but a man's reach should exceed his grasp, or what's a heaven for?"[354] There are a plethora of definitions for ambition, with no sure answer. But it was Henry Wadsworth Longfellow who said, 'If you would hit the mark, you must aim a little above it; every arrow that flies feels the attraction of earth.'

It certainly involves effort, for Jennie Jerome Churchill said to her son, 'You seem to have no real purpose in life and won't realise at the age of twenty-two that for a man life means work, and hard work if you mean to succeed.'[355] Condoleezza Rice, former US secretary of state and national security advisor was thirty-eight when she became Stanford University's youngest and first female provost. She was a gifted pianist who began studying at Alabama's Birmingham Conservatory at age ten. She became an accomplished ice skater, rising at 4.30 a.m. to spend two hours at the rink before school.

There are usually early signs in a person's life of what lies ahead of them. Bill Clinton, former US president and current global celebrity, at age sixteen, beat 1,000 other boys to win a mock state senate seat and a trip to Washington. He then got himself into a position of shaking hands with his idol, John F. Kennedy. Oprah Winfrey could read at the age of two and, when she started school, insisted she begin in the first grade. The next year, she was put in the third grade. She now heads a billion-dollar media empire, which includes movies, a magazine, and a successful TV network and production studio, HARPO.

Tiger Woods, at age six, listened to motivational tapes – 'I will make my own destiny' – while practicing his swing in the mirror. At twenty-one, he was the youngest golfer ever to be ranked number one in the world. At thirty, he held the record for the most prize money won in a career. Michael Schumacher, who had eighty-four wins and seven world championship titles and was the most successful Formula One driver of all time raced go-karts from the age of four. He became the local club champion at six and German junior champion at fifteen.

As Jeffrey Kluger, senior writer at *Time* magazine noted, 'A fire in the belly doesn't light itself. Does the spark of ambition lie in the genes, family, culture – or even your own hands?' Is there an adequate answer? No one is quite sure, but it is certain that 'Ambition is so powerful a passion in the human breast that however high we reach, we are never satisfied.'[356] Grow up in a rich family, and you can either use your inherited wealth and position as a tool for further life success or become slothful, living off other people's ambition. Be born into a poor family, and your poverty can be the underlying motivation to lift yourself higher, or it can sponsor the inertia of hopelessness. It seems there are no set rules to say which family will produce achievers. But to many, failure is a trial of great proportions. It causes sorrow and bitter jealousy, for self-worth is a tyrant. Our future seems dismal and unfulfilled. Regret dogs our footsteps. Life in the slow lane challenges our confidence.

Paul the Apostle said, 'But I press on, that I may lay hold of that for which Christ Jesus has also laid hold of me. ...but one thing I do, forgetting those things which are behind and reaching forward to those things which are ahead, I press toward the goal for the prize of the upward call of God in Christ Jesus.'[357] Here was his ambition, clearly stated. With God on your side, it doesn't matter which family you have been born into, because now you are *His* child and in *His* family. In *His* genes lies success. But be careful how you define success, lest you find yourself diverted by expectation.

Ambition is good for a person, but it is important to ensure that that objective is centred round conveying kingdom health all around and especially within. It was Adolf Hitler who said, 'With a suitcase full of clothes and underwear in my hand and an indomitable will in my heart, I set out for Vienna.... I too hope to become "something".' He did. His ambition killed 50 million people. But Jesus has saved far more, and He continues to give life. As we let our ambition swell in God, it can only bring good.

Two babies in the womb of Old Testament Rebecca were in strife, and Jacob took hold of Esau's heel, in the original meaning 'to trip'. And this is the description of Jacob until God meets him at Jabbok; he was always trying to trip someone up and gain the advantage. His natural cunning was the confusion of his life, yet God loved him. Even before birth, God had determined that the elder should serve the younger, not because of favouritism but because of choice. Jacob had the right value judgment. It seemed that the pre-birth tension became the postnatal variance, as brothers divided in character, desires, and values lived out a family relationship in rage and deceit.

God declared His will in the lives of these two brothers from their beginning. Yet Isaac tried to alter the divine edict, and Jacob tried to take, before its time, the promise that was his. If we know God's will yet it seems too distant and physically impossible, we tend to supplement God with acts that prove He needs us. We often bring disaster on ourselves, and we may well finish up serving sheep. We find it difficult to settle down and wait for God to make bread from stones and tend to believe that the age of miracles is now past when God is dealing with us.

Our plans and problem

When we *cannot* wait for God, we will probably *have* to wait for God. Patience is the key that opens the door into the pastures of God, and He allows endurance free reign to prove it. Someone once said, 'Beware of egging God on.'[358] If we do, His goodness could be our bane and ultimately our blame. Never force God to meet your plans; doing so may forever silence you in the kingdom, for your mouth may become so full of good things that it chokes you. Our desires may make us too stout for God so that that we cannot effectively run the race, and we will forever be panting with exertion rather than devotion.

Man forever wants to see the end at the beginning. Adam looked for it in the Garden of Eden and found that kind of knowledge was fatal. It was in fact a 'fatal attraction'. Christians are forever peering into the prophetic scope of their tomorrows with impatience at today's discipline; whereas it is only the ignorance of the future that makes the 'now' bearable, it could get worse! But, we have this consolation; the 'worse' of Calvary was followed by the dawn of redemption and the restoration of glory. The place of the skull is the prelude to the steps of the throne.

Esau sought with tears to repent of his folly, but his past decision was irretrievable. So it was with Abraham, who had to live with Ishmael, much to his chagrin. Our decisions can often affect our lifestyle and our destiny, and there is the possibility that we will never be what God wants us to be. Time is often too short for God to redeem the folly we have caused, and He has to appoint and anoint another. God cannot wait forever to bring His kingdom in, and if our choices are always gauged by sensual satisfaction, then God will have the difficulty of accomplishing His purposes through unworthy vessels.

Our destiny may be changed to fit in with our conception of divine grace and its demands on us. If we cannot raise ourselves to the level of faith to value the birthright of God, then we must forever live in the family of God as second-born sons. We will, of course, take less than we should have done. But don't blame God. Often the red lentils of the necessary and the legitimate are acquisitions that we secure at the expense of our spiritual heritage.

When good men sin, they usually do it well!

If virtuous men fall into sin, then they will usually excel at it, for they use the same dedication as they had to righteousness to debase themselves. That is why tall men in the kingdom fall the furthest because they are good at whatever they do. When Jacob deceived his father, he did it sufficiently well to confuse the old man, who knew his elder son more than any other, or so he thought.

A family called of God does not mean that they are a family who live by kingdom rules. The partiality of Isaac and Rebekah towards the two sons, Esau and Jacob, was compromisingly wrong and was one of the factors that contributed to the whole of this unfortunate saga. In fact, the home conditions made it easier to perpetrate the false scheme. That in itself should be a salutary reminder of how easy it is to ferment trouble by attitudes in the home. Our Christianity must invade family relationships, or else it will result in disaster in many different ways.

One would expect that Esau would get the revelation and Jacob the darkness, for, after all, Esau had been supplanted. However, God's purpose supersedes our moral judgments, and He will come to any man who *genuinely* wants to know Him and His ways. Esau robbed himself of his greatest blessing by stealing immediate pleasure. The natural was elevated above the supernatural, and the mess of pottage became the symbol of his slavery. We are bound to what dominates us, and if our strong desires rule supreme, we will only become carnal kings.

Jacob, although running from his misdemeanours, wanted things spiritual, hence his stealing of the birthright. And he found that his point of departure from truth became the opportunity for commission into God's will. God can turn upside down any vagrancies on our part and make them into something special. He does not approve of our methods, but He does seem to reward spiritual zeal; after all, there are so many Christians who are lukewarm and apathetic about spiritual values and so devoid of ambition that one wonders, in the present church, how God can ever bring the kingdom in.

Jacob immediately turned his pillow into a pillar and made Bethel a special place, but there is a danger; we tend to limit God to one place only. If we are forever thinking of Bethel's ladder, we will always fail, for God is not confined to either geography or rungs. He will meet us at any point and in any way of our escape to bring us into line with the divine plan, and we should be careful not to be too carried away and sanctify that place above all others like a shrine to be venerated. The problem with some Christians is that they saw their ladder so long ago that the rungs have now rotted!

God knows were the gold is

As a divine prospector, God knows where to dig. Gold is often found in the most unlikely places, but to him that has eyes to see, the barren place becomes a mine of inestimable wealth. We would tend not to glance at a man twice in our summation of his worth and use for God, yet lying just beneath the surface are those qualities that God needs and knows are there. History is a pageant of God doing the *miraculous* with the *unlikely* in order to achieve the *impossible*. King David was such a man. The prophet saw what God saw, and he was anointed. When the woman with an alabaster box of precious ointment came to anoint Jesus' feet, the assembled men saw a prostitute. But Jesus saw a woman.

God picks up one man and puts down another, not out of caprice but discernment. Men and women would, if left to their human judgment, flock to Esau with his strong, sensual, generous ways – every inch a leader. Yet God chose Jacob, the tent dweller and domestic chef who twisted himself into the divine destiny.

The linking is laughable

When God chose to link His name with that of Jacob, there must have been amazement in heaven. If we were choosing a man with whom God could identify, as a union of heaven and earth, it is doubtful whether we would have even shortlisted the patriarch. Perhaps Abraham, God's friend, or Moses, the meekest man on earth, or even Daniel of lion fame. Well, these are obvious candidates. But Jacob? He stole the birthright at seventy years of age, and at that advanced stage in his life, there was no way that he could change. A mindset and life had been established. The psychologists would say his case was hopeless.

Compare these two texts: 'thou worm Jacob' and 'the God of Jacob'. What a contrast. Yet God can join the two by an act of pursuit that never left him alone until he came to his senses and made that effort to confirm the word of faith and promise with a corresponding lifestyle. God's dedication is an act of the divine until the human is established.

It is said of Jacob that 'he served sheep for a wife.'[359] So did Jesus! And unless Jesus had died for them, Jacob would have got the better bargain. Any man who could work for fourteen years to secure a bride must have exceptional love. If God could use that kind of devotion on the human level and transfer it into the spiritual realm, what a man He would have. It is this glimpse of Jacob's consistency that reveals why God chose him. Whatever he did, he did it well, whether it was scheming or living. God can use that kind of dedication.

The strongest point

The thigh is the strongest point of a man's body, and with this, he throws his assailant. It was not strange, therefore, that God poked Jacob's thigh, and he limped into blessing. He became shrivelled in his flesh to reveal what he had been in the spirit. God will always take our strongest point and make it our place of weakness, lest we boast of our own effort. Some men are too strong for God; He has to wait until their human resources begin to fail before He can use them. Your disability may, therefore, become His ability. Jacob was eventually crippled into commitment after struggling against the inevitable but not the impossible. The angel was all he could handle, not *more* than he could handle, and that was the right handle to grasp!

Chapter 18

Dusk

It was that inevitable walking time, the time that dog owners look forward to twice a day, as they relentlessly stride around an appropriate field – all in the pursuit of exercise. The monotonous routine day in and day out is sometimes mind-numbingly boring. But this day was different. There was a new sign up in the park – 'This Park closes at dusk.' *Dusk*, I thought. *What time is that?*

I asked my wife, and she said, 'We all know when that is.'

'Perhaps we all do,' I replied. 'But when precisely is it?'

'You look in the paper, and it tells you there,' she answered.

'Yes,' I said. 'But what time is dusk today?'

'Well, I don't know, I haven't looked.'

'So, before you leave the house each day, you have to scan the paper to check when dusk is. Should that be necessary?'

'I don't need to, as I don't walk in the park.'

'But you should. It's good for you.'

'I don't need to because you do.'

So the *discussion* rolled on!

It made me think of definitions and twilight. I've never really thought of dusk, and I believe the park authorities are somewhat naive in putting that notice up, because to the majority of the people, it is meaningless. Dusk could be any time depending on the cloud cover, and if you have to remove your parked car before the park closes the gates, you may miss it by a few seconds and leave it until next day – not a nice thought.

In the twilight of uncertainty, there is a gradual waning of God's revelation in personal lives, until folk are just living noticeably in a state of half-light, which is twilight. Twilight is nothingness; it is neither one nor the other and is indeterminate. It has no clarity, it hovers in a no-man's land, bringing the thought that, perhaps something ought to be done, but then again perhaps it could wait a little longer. Car drivers never quite know when to put their lights on in the twilight. People like twilight because they need not make decisions. They can argue it is an unknown time, and, therefore, clear answers needn't be given.

There comes a time that is a period of twilight in many people's lives – a time when the sun begins to set on their lives. And this is particularly illustrated in the case of Moses. His life's desire was for the twilight of existence, with no harsh light of destiny. God had other ideas. The backside of the desert was the heart side of God and was not his buffer or stop; it was merely a long pause, and there was quite a journey yet ahead. This was but the thoroughfare and training ground. Forty years remained for Moses to play the most important part of God's journey in shaping the nation of Israel.

Later that month, another notice was put in park. It read, 'This park closes at 4.30 p.m.' Someone had at last discovered the ambiguity and corrected it. We now knew when the park closed. We could now make an accurate decision about when to leave, whether we read the paper or not. That is like God. He never leaves us in doubt. His word is clear and unambiguous. 'The wages of sin is death, but the gift of God is eternal life.'[360] Short, simple clear. Here is another one: 'For God loved the world that he gave his only begotten son.'[361] There is no doubt about that; it is supreme, unmatched divine love – love for you and me.

The Bible is replete with clear guidelines for life. There is no twilight with scripture. God wants us to know and know clearly His divine will. He puts up His notices so that He does not have to correct them later on. '*Oh, taste and see that the* LORD *is good; blessed is the man who trusts in Him.*[362] Simply trust in magnificent blessing – undeniable and unlimited. God is positive, not hesitant. There is no twilight with God. He wants us to be the same. Imbibe the Word, absorb the Spirit, and live in the light.

However, there is another situation that arises in nature that needs our consideration. It is midday – noon by another name. It's a question of 'midday madness' – 'nor for the pestilence that walks in darkness; nor for the destruction that wastes at noonday.'[363]

'There is a peril in the garish day.'[364] This thought is a seed point; from it, we develop this chapter for our hearts in our individual Christian life and close the book. In the zenith of the day, when the sun has gilded all things and the heart is surfeited with the goodness, *the adder emerges in the brightness.* Troubles and trials come. That is to be expected. But under another guise, when we are at the height of our blessing, there can come a subtlety that could destroy us.

As spring gives way to summer, there spreads a malaise that sprouts lethargy. In the tropics, people just stand and stare at noontime, and life seems to stop. Only mad dogs and English men go out in the midday sun! Hidden in the apparent goodness of the heat can come the onset of disease; that is why inoculations are important. It seems so delightful, as the sunlight touches all things and beautifies them, even rubbish tips! However, lingering in the rays of warmth can come yellow fever, typhoid, and cholera.

In the midday of our success, either in the world or the Christian life, can come the enemies of our life. It is a time that can be fraught with danger, and witnesses of every generation hang in the gallery of fallen heroes. The greatest hour of Christ was hung in darkness by His Father. In all walks of life, through every phase of either failure or success, comes temptation. Most books concentrate on failure, disenchantment, distress, danger, and catastrophe but fail to point out the possibility of failure in triumph.

Things cannot be seen clearly in the brightness of that hour

A destruction can waste us away at noonday! Harbouring in that glare can come the uncertainty of a distant horizon that misdirects vision. Shapes become distorted and shimmer in the distance, and only what is near is sharp and in focus. Our long sight is affected, and we are so taken with the immediate that we lose sight of possible vantage and direction points. Those points are what keep us on the route. There are times when we must be prepared to turn, but the sign is too blurred, and we pass it while we are occupied with the local terrain. When the sun awakes after the long night of the winter, there is this tendency to forget all things and just stand in its warming rays. Important issues are neglected, and sun worshipping dominates the programme. The now must never displace tomorrow, and our present success must not occupy all our time. Jesus is God's horizon, for the horizon is where heaven and earth met, and this is always in Jesus.

A child will be so taken with the toy department that he or she loses his or her guardian in the crush of the superstore. Tinsel replaces real values for the moment. That is the subtle peril of life's brilliant noon. We can be so engrossed that we miss God. The glitter of gold can make us forget the glory of God – not God, but the glory of God, His living presence that sanctifies and moderates all we do. The thrill of success can tarnish our relationship with God. The possession of our possessions can dislocate our place in the body, the church of Christ.

Abraham got lost when he tarried in Haran. He did not move out into the Promised Land until God took his father and turned his noonday into midnight. Jacob, having reached his ascendancy, returned with his fortune, wives, and animals. But he lost sight of God's protection and started tricking again. David's sunshine was cloud-riven as his child, the son of profligacy, was taken from him. His noontime of wealth, power, and popularity were soon to be shaken, as he lost sight of goodness and purity. Judas sat in such light that he lost all sense of value and sold Jesus for a paupers' price.

In the noontide, there is a diminishing of moisture

The beginning of drought sets in. The fierce heat shrinks things, and rivers, ponds, and fountains begin to dry up and falter in their flow. Stiffness ensues as the hardpan of the earth's crust becomes baked and unyielding. In a spiritual sense, our sympathies begin to run low and there comes an austerity of feelings. The empty riverbed is mindful of our barren emotions, as we no longer sympathise with our fellows who are passing through the valley of tears, trying to make it a verdant pasture for growth.

When there are no clouds in our sky, we find it hard to remember the darkness of the storm that threatens others. If we are never sick, we will forever name it and claim it like the hyper faith ministry. They teach that through faith we can have all things, but life and expereicne is not like that. If we feel no pain, exhaustion, or feebleness, we won't appreciate such feelings in others. We could impatiently brush them to one side and vigorously pursue our ambitions. David the king was incensed at Nathan's example of exploitation, not realising it was himself the prophet was referring to.[365]

Defeat makes us very sympathetic. Too much victory and we cannot remember what it was like to stumble and fall. Thus, being overcomers, we can become insensitive to others and so become alienated from our fellow man. 'And be kind to one another, tenderhearted, forgiving one another, just as God in Christ forgave you.'[366] Joseph, sold into slavery and then promoted to the right hand of Pharaoh, could have developed a brusque and insensitive spirit. But when his brothers who sold him came on the scene, he was moved with compassion. 'So shall ye say unto Joseph, Forgive, I pray thee now, the trespass of thy brethren, and their sin; for they did unto thee evil: and now, we pray thee, forgive the trespass of the servants of the God of thy father. And Joseph wept when they spake unto him.'[367]

Ruth and Naomi came from the fields of Moab. Naomi, having left Bethlehem in midst of famine, found that Boaz, who stayed in the famine, welcomed and spoke kindly to them. They needed help and found it in the near kinsman who understood the situation. He was touched with their infirmities, for his riches did not alter his compassion. 'Then she said, Let me find favour in thy sight, my lord; for that you have comforted me, and for that you have spoken friendly unto your handmaid.'[368] And later, we read, 'And Naomi said unto her daughter in law, blessed be he of the Lord, who hath not left off his kindness to the living and to the dead.'[369] Boaz had been through the awful famine that resided in that area for the decade Naomi had been away and knew the rigours of poverty and starvation. He appreciated their penury and spoke kindly to their hearts. He was sensitive to their condition.

It was God Himself who visited earth as Jesus. 'Through the tender mercy of our God; whereby the dayspring from on high hath visited us.'[370] He became, as Romans 1:3 says, 'made of the seed of David according to the flesh.' The glory of heaven never became too bright that God missed us in our extremity. The humanity of Jesus linked us with heaven.

Pyramids of dew

Gilbert White, a celebrated chronicler of the eighteenth century, made it his interest to understand and investigate the collecting of dew.[371] The earth's atmosphere contains 13,000 cubic kilometres of water vapour at any one time, which is six times as much as in all the world's rivers. This prospect sets up a challenge for scientists to maximise earth's resources. It is a tantalising prize for would-be inventors.

Dew is the term for small droplets of water that appear on thin objects in the morning or evening. Dew results from atmospheric moisture that condenses after a warm day and appears during the night on cooled surfaces as small drops. The cool surfaces cool the nearby air, decreasing the amount of humidity (dissolved moisture) the local air can hold. The extra vapour condenses (precipitates out of solution in the air).

During White's time, the southeast of England was dotted with dew ponds, most of them dug to capture some rain, but were also designed to condense moisture from the air. Straw was put beneath the clay bottom of the ponds. This insulated the water, keeping it colder than the soil at night, and a layer of stones ensured that the pond shed heat quickly, lowering the temperature further.

Technology has now enabled a weather modification technique called cloud seeding. Silver iodide is sprayed into clouds, turning droplets into rainfall. And catching fog also has a proven track record. On a ridge in the rainless Atacama Desert in northern Chile, there are tattered remains of large sheets of plastic mesh that once harvested water from the fogs that rolled in from the Pacific Ocean. These twelve-by-thirteen-metre nets caught 150 litres a day, filling taps in the nearby fishing village of Chungungo.

Apparently, the last traditional English dew pond digger retired in the 1930s, but in other places, like Lanzarote, the farmers still mulch their vines with a volcanic ash that condenses night-time moisture to water the crops. And Frederich Zibold, a Russian engineer stumbled across some Crimean pyramids whilst clearing some trees. Apparently as the sea breezes blew in at night, they filtered through these pyramid stones, condensing sufficient water for 80,000 inhabitants.

Poets have turned lyrical in their descriptions of the dew – 'the dew-bead, Gem of earth and sky-begotten' (George Elliot) and "stars of morning, dew-drops, which the sun impearls on every leaf and flower" (Milton). But whatever the language, century, or civilisation, humankind has always endeavoured to harness nature's natural moisture and use it for the maintenance of life.

In the spiritual realm, God speaks of the benefit of the dew. Isaac's blessing upon Jacob was, 'God give thee of the dew of heaven.'[372] Dew is a heavenly gift. The poetic language of man is only superseded by that of the Bible – 'For God's light of life will fall like dew upon them!'[373] Dew is gentle and it imparts life, just as light shines without any weight or disturbance. Mount Hermon rises from an impenetrable swamp, where the boiling vapour, under the rays of the sun, ascends until it touches the snowy sides of the mountain, and condenses, drenching everything. Travellers have commented upon the significance of the heaviness of the dew; it is so substantial as to be almost unique. So too is God's blessing.

When the night is clearer and the moon brighter, dew drenches the fields longer, and it takes only a short time of the night for the dew to replace the moisture of the earth, which it had taken all day for the sun to dry up. The dew is an image of the Paraclete, the Holy Spirit, who sweetly descends upon the soul of the saint. Often in the 'dark night of the soul', God will send His Spirit as dew to replace the energy absorbed by the heart of the daytime trial. He also sends his moon to lighten some of the way. The secret I learned in life's pain is to collect a dew pond and drink regularly of its sweetness. It is, indeed, the secret place of victory.

To gain the full import of the blessing of divine dew, we must turn to Proverbs 19:12. 'The king's favour is as the dew upon the grass.' For 'favour', read *pleasure*. It is God's joy to cascade upon us the moisture of the Spirit. In fact, why not make it your life's ambition, like George White did, to harness the dew? When trials come, in the dry season, imbibe from that divine pool daily, especially at noontide.

There is a tendency to have ambition without aspiration

The danger in life is the possibility of pushing towards a goal without a thought for refinement or spiritual elevation – getting on, not up. As has been said, a cow will crush a thousand wild flowers to reach water. Nothing will stop it once the scent has been caught. Even in spiritual realms, people are motivated by thoughts of power; every effort focuses on attaining the desired position, without sense that it is God's arm that makes the promotion. It is the strength of our own purpose that prevails. It has push but no worship.

Jacob broke 1,000 rules to get the promise. He became a passionate example of winning at all costs. His sun was rising in the sky. His ambition was rising higher. But the precision of God's timing was forgotten in the rush for dominance. 'The successful man is prone to magnify might without reference to right.'[374] Cain destroyed Abel because he assumed his sun was up.

What can I do?

Seek shelter in God 'He that dwells in the secret place of the most high shall abide under the shadow of the almighty. I will say of the Lord, he is my refuge and my fortress: my God; in him will I trust' [375]

This then is the answer. When the three goodly young men were thrown into the furnace, there was a fourth that walked with them. 'He answered and said, Lo, I see four men loose, walking in the midst of the fire, and they have no hurt; and the form of the fourth is like the Son of God.'[376] In the heat of that hour, when we reach our midday, Jesus will walk with us. Hallelujah! As we hide in Him, the secret place becomes the sure place of victory. He anoints our eyes so that the shimmer of the heat haze does not befoul our vision with self-importance. The glorious triumph of Calvary was turned into darkness at midday so that victory was measured in pain and suffering. Keep the Calvary spirit uppermost in your heart as success approaches and never let the world fool you into thinking that your *noonday* is your *eternal day.*

Time passes, and so does success, which is only man-made. Remember it is those who 'dwell' in the secret place who are covered. Dwelling is different from visiting intermittently. Some Christians use God as they do their holidays; He's there for two weeks a year. He only becomes popular when the evening of our experience comes.

Chapter 19

Broken Footrests (Hosea 2:6–7)

Sebastian Horsley went to the Philippines to join their Easter crucifixion ceremonies. He paid £2,000 to be crucified so he could heighten his artistic sense by pushing himself to the 'extreme of suffering'. Each year, the Filipinos *mimic* Christ's death to pay for their sins. This year, Sebastian decided to experience the real thing. Due to an accident, it turned out to be an overwhelming painful experience. They strapped his arms and wrists to the cross and supported his feet on a platform and then drove five-inch nails through his palms into the timber cross member. Apparently the pain was so excruciating that, although he tried to concentrate on beautiful things, he drifted in and out of consciousness.

Each year, at this ceremony on the island of San Fernando, ten people volunteer to atone for their sins by mimicking Jesus' death on the cross. They are scourged with whips and dragged through the streets before arriving at a 'Calvary', with three crosses on a hill. They remain on the crosses for thirty minutes, with three women in attendance. Before their crucifixion, they have to sign a waiver taking full responsibly for whatever psychological and or physiological consequences might arise from their actions.

In Horsley's case, the foot support collapsed; the straps broke, and he was left hanging by his nail-riven hands. He slipped into unconsciousness and darkness and was revived by a fellow artist who had travelled with him. The locals stemmed the flow of blood by putting their fingers in the wounds.

Although he suffered no permanent long-term medical problems, his hands were bandaged for months after the self-imposed suffering. He said after the ordeal, 'An artist has to go to every extreme, to stretch his sensibility through excess and suffering to feel and to communicate more.' He also added, 'At times I think it was reckless; at other times poetic.'[377]

I have never met anyone who thinks suffering is poetic, but people often believe that God is irresponsible in allowing the trial to come and to continue! Some people can look at the bright side of any adversity; instead of grumbling, they are full of grace. To us Christians, problems should be the stepping stones to greater maturity, not a slew of despondency, which they so often are. Too often, we believe that God is punishing us for waywardness but cannot think of anything we have done to merit His wrath. However, there are times we walk out of God's will and need a gentle push to get us back on track, and God has many ways of doing this; unfortunately, some are painful, although temperate in proportion to response.

Joseph was innocent while untested but virtuous after he had refused Potiphar's wife. God is good at arranging situations that can challenge us to prove our blameless profession. As we strive to be like Christ in our daily living, our faith will be tested to extremes. And often we will feel like Sebastian Horsley – only we didn't volunteer for it. And our foot supports collapse too often.

The parable of Israel

One of God's greatest parables is the nation of Israel. They represent God's winning ways as he endeavours to lead them out of thraldom into freedom and their inbuilt resistance to his wooing, repeatedly going after strange gods and playing fast and loose with Him. God, therefore, employs varied means to keep them loyal and to expose their fidelity or infidelity to His commandments and guidance, as

He can with us in our pilgrimage. I hesitated when it came to how I would present the parable of Israel. I feared most readers would assume the Israelites trials are a result of their faithful lifestyle and dedication to the faith, but it might not be so; there could be a worm in the apple! We all like to believe that we do believe and that our walk is blameless, but Israel manifests continual waywardness and God's ability to correct that error. It could happen to us. Our error could cause us pain; this may not be obvious.

The Old Testament book of Hosea informs us of this allegorically, speaking in terms of a bad marriage. And as marriage is rooted in the minds of most people, the message presented is a clear one. The prophet marries Gomer at God's behest and finds that she is a nymphomaniac, running after other men. Hosea was tested to his limit, like God has been for generations with Israel and now with the church who is to be His bride (and we, as individuals of faith, are part of that company). We, at times, also test Him, I think to distraction, if that were possible. Revelation chapters 2 and 3 illustrate this. We can act like Gomer, running after worldly allurements to the soul.

The Bible is replete with figurative examples of spiritual truth and instructs our mind simply by graphic examples that elucidate truth, which forcibly lays hold of our thoughts. For instance, the relationship between God and the Jews rates highly as the continuous parable as any other story in our understanding. Their repeated spiritual adultery shows God's patience and promise-keeping to His covenant with them – *an example of the waywardness of man and the pursuing love of God*. 'For whatsoever things were written aforetime were written for our learning, that we through patience and comfort of the scriptures might have hope.'[378] Thus, this allegory is relevant for us today. Let us not dismiss history as extraneous but accept it is full of divine meaning for twenty-first-century living. God's dealing with Israel will not be different from us, for we are His church, and they, like us, are part of his legacy and divine will.

It needs little interpretation, for the word he gives has a precise meaning; His action against them is like a fence that contains, restricts, and protects. This fence is designed to shut in and also to shut out, to entwine so they were caught in restraint but also confined for their protection. But He says specifically of Israel, 'And now, please let Me tell you what I will do to My vineyard: I will take away its hedge, and it shall be burned; and break down its wall, and it shall be trampled down.'[379] Job had such a hedge that thwarted Satan: 'Have You not made a hedge around him, around his household, and around all that he has on every side?'[380] The answer is yes; God had, and no one could penetrate that barrier unless he agreed. We likewise are safely shut up for our protection and His providence. When God removed it from Job, Satan came rushing in with his fury.

Thus it was with Israel. Because they abused their relationship with God, He took away their protection, so the parable is of the husbandman who fences his crops and cattle in with a prickly hedge, the pricklier the better, to keep out the intruder and to safely protect his charges. The sharper the better, so conversely, if they break out and wander away, they will feel the briars by the torn flesh and blood.

Our text adds this, 'and make a wall, that she shall not find her paths.'[381] Like Israel, we may break through the hedge of briars that ensures our security and come out bleeding and wounded into the wilderness of the world. Thus, our foolishness may be hampered by God with insuperable barriers of difficulty. Jeremiah laments the waywardness of Israel: 'Your own wickedness will correct you, and your apostasies will reprove you; know therefore and see that it is evil and bitter. For you to forsake the LORD your God, and the dread of Me is not in you.'[382] God can, therefore, deprive them of their freedom, taking away the desires of their eyes and thwarting their enterprises and schemes. God can drop upon them afflictions like thunder and rain according to their moral perversion. Consequently, they will return to their first love and seek God again, like the prodigal in the New Testament.

The comparison is necessary, for considering what we once were and what are now, what we once enjoyed and what we lack now, it's the basis of repentance and reconciliation. The son in Luke 15 wasted his substance, destroyed his reputation, and reduced himself to an abject condition. He fed on husks but remembered the honour in which he once was held. He came to himself and, in doing that, came to the father.

These Old and New Testament stories tell us that it is easy to go away from God, for no one can boast in their righteousness. Israel was chosen to have the benefit of His overall guidance, provision, and love. Yet abusing that favour, they followed other gods, and the son, loved by a dear father, yet descended into debauchery. In Israel's case, God worked twofold, confining the Israelites by fences and walls, thus restricting them, or breaking down the physical barriers so they could suffer attack by wild animals and their enemies. God is saying that, if we go away from Him, He will deal with us appropriately to bring us back. But when we do return, there will be a welcome and blessing. *God can use all means to establish His love for us.*

His love extends past our failings and unfaithfulness; His word and pledge are constant. He may allow trials and tribulations to come but, with them, turn our hearts towards home. He also promises, 'I will never leave or forsake you.'[383] Even with that promise, there is still a tendency or proneness to go astray. For we can transfer to the creature what ought to be placed upon the creator. We love, fear, and trust other things and people in preference to God. Thus, these things become our idols and our lovers that we chase after. Our declensions are not gross acts of immorality necessarily, and unfaithfulness sears our minds because of misplaced trust. Our deviations can be mental, not physical, so our hearts are drawn away from the purity of faith that pleases God. 'Do not love the world or the things in the world. If anyone loves the world, the love of the Father is not in him.'[384]

However, this action of drawing us back by His omnipotent actions of love, mistaken by us, is a sign of His kindness. For He doesn't give us up but watches like the New Testament father. His tolerance and forgiveness are grand examples of eternal tenderness. It says of Ephraim that he is 'joined unto idols let him alone'.[385] And what an indictment that is – utter finality, no future hope. But in this generation, God bears and forbears with an extravagant forgiveness that surprises the most ardent of wasters. He could destroy us and vindicate His righteousness, but instead, He employs means to bring us back into the fold of mercy. Shout it from the housetops! Our text says, 'And she shall seek them, but shall not find them' – seeking the paths that lead to her lovers. But God confuses the way so that, in that puzzlement, people see the clear way back to God.

The scriptures say quite plainly, 'What is man that You are mindful of him, and the son of man that You visit him?'[386] And, frankly, we are not much to be mindful of, but He still encourages our fellowship. And in our down-sitting and uprising, He is there. He provides new mercies each morning and 'songs in the night'. His overflowing grace is sufficient to convince us that His love and His way is the best route. Absalom, who was twice ignored, set fire to the field that was adjacent to get Joab's attention. And when God wants our attention, He has innumerable ways and methods of catching it. *Trials, tribulations, and sufferings can be just part of His plan.* The prophet's voice rings today as yesteryear: 'And turn you not aside: for then should you go after vain things, which cannot profit nor deliver; for they are vain.'[387] Often our fretting is because we cannot get our way. For our way is often against God, who withstands us so He can get *His* way. This is God's way of *preventing us disappointment in eternity.* How sad it would be if we were to have no sheaves in eternity – no harvest when we could have had a full barn. People too often forget eternity's tomorrow.

It can always be the New Year

New Year's resolutions persist, and this would always be mine – that God's people will recapture a love for Jesus and reflect it in their lifestyle irrespective of oppositions and innumerable burdens. There are many necessary things in life, but our commitment to Jesus Christ should be the highest, for it is through Him that we have salvation. It was John Wesley who said, 'Beware you be not swallowed up in books; an ounce of love is worth a pound of knowledge.' In this Google age of unlimited knowledge, many Christians will be swamped with an abundance of facts concerning the Christ. Thus, they will have contact but possibly not communion and never really connect in love with the Saviour. It was the Shulamite maiden who said, 'The king has brought me into his chambers.... We will be glad and rejoice in You. We will remember your love more than wine.'[388] In the book, *Jesus Manifesto*, by Leonard Sweet and Frank Viola the writers state, "There is a 'gotcha moment'"[389] when Jesus gets you for life.' And you 'begin to live out of Jesus-love.' It was George Matheson who penned a great hymn sung mostly in yesteryears:

> O love that wilt not let me go
> I rest my weary soul in Thee;
> I give Thee back the life I owe
> That in Thine ocean depths its flow
> May richer, fuller be.

Steve Green sings a moving melody that contains these lines, which echo George Matheson in a contemporary mode: 'To love the Lord our God is the heartbeat of our mission the spring from which ours service overflows.'

A poignant message in tongues was delivered at the end of one of our advent services and from memory this is what it said.

This Advent season, you have brought out your tree; clothed it in baubles, tinsel, trimmings and lights; and placed your gifts around it. Then you take it down and store it for another year, to bring it out again and live in this process in succeeding years. But there is another tree, which has no baubles but does have red blood, no tinsel but a crown of thorns, no fairy lights except the Light of the World hung there. Upon this, the Saviour died, and this tree should not be taken down and hidden for eleven months and brought out again for a new season, for every day, this tree is the power source of life. 'But now you who were once far off have been brought nigh by the blood of Christ.'[390] We cannot or should not put this tree away, for it is a continual sacrifice, operating as we are daily cleansed.

My heart was stirred, my love flowed, my desire was ignited for a stricken Saviour who had been heightened amid the celebratory forecasts of the future. And all things were put into an eternal perspective through an overwhelming love for Jesus, like the women in the New Testament who broke through race, riches, and religion to weep, wash, and wipe the feet of Jesus. We can impersonate a worshipper and lover of God, but we cannot impart what we do not possess. Eventually, our inward reality becomes our outward reality, and we reap what we sow. If our public presentation isn't the same as our private one, God will often make our private public. We must support God in all His ways in our lives as a testimony of His great faithfulness. To do that, we must learn to dwell in the sanctuary of His love.

Many Bible colleges today teach management and business studies to prospective ministers and make them good at organisation, planning, and control. But we are supposed to be priests of the holy presence. Those two functions can be separated, and Jesus did precisely that – 'Mary has chosen the better part.'[391] Our time at His feet should outweigh our time preparing our flow chart; why do carrots dominate when we can adore the matchless lamb?

As C. S. Lewis wrote, 'Though our feelings come and go, God's love for us does not.' Our love will vacillate with the seasons, the surrounding circumstances, the ferocity of the trial, the darkness of night's despair, the raging of the tempest, the swelling of the tide, and the deluge of adversity – *but for God*! And that is sufficient.

We must take to heart the words of this hymn by J. W. Van De Venter:

> I never, no, never will leave him,
> Grow weary of service and grieve him,
> I'll constantly trust and believe him,
> Remain in his presence divine;
> Abiding in love ever flowing,
> In knowledge and grace ever growing,
> Confiding implicitly, knowing
> That Jesus the Saviour is mine. [Refrain]

Chapter 20

Spin Doctoring

*And he said unto me, My grace is sufficient for thee: for my strength
is made perfect in weakness. Most gladly therefore will I rather glory
in my infirmities, that the power of Christ may rest upon me.*
—2 Corinthians 12:9, KJV

The ultimate reality

Daniel Defoe, author of *Robinson Crusoe* in 1719, was put in the
pillory between 29 and 31 July 1703 because of a tract he published.
His intention in producing the leaflet was to make it look as if a
foaming high Anglican zealot of the most bigoted stamp had written
it. Drawing on High Church sermons, the pamphlet argued that the
best way of dealing with the dissenters was to banish them abroad
and send their preachers to the hangman. The Church of England,
it argued, is like Christ crucified between two thieves, Papists on the
one side and Nonconformist sectarians on the other. Very well, let us
crucify the thieves. To go on tolerating them is like allowing a plague
to continue without medical treatment.

The authorities were not amused and they offered a reward for
information on the perpetrator, having discovered from the printer
who had done it. DeFoe was soon arrested in Sptialfields and
imprisoned in Newgate gaol. At his trial, he pleaded guilty and was

sentenced to three one-hour periods in the pillory. The pillory was used to punish minor criminals, including cheats, liars, rioters, and homosexuals, by shaming them in public.

Some of the candidates were killed or maimed for life as the crowd pelted them with eggs, fruit, dead cats and dogs, every variety of filth, stones, saucepans, and other suitable missiles. Fortunately for Defoe, he was pilloried when it rained, which kept down the crowds, and all that was thrown at him were flowers from his friends.

His brickworks failed, he could not pay his fine, and he was returned to Newgate Prison. However, four months later the government paid his fine from secret service funds. They realised his worth as a spin doctor, and within a year, he was employed to publish a regular newspaper, which showed the ministry in a favourable light, and to act as a government spy. He continued for many years, spreading propaganda for successive ministries, and it was not until later he turned to writing fiction. Fiction is what spin doctoring really is; it spins tales around truth to deceive. 'Propaganda is that branch of the art of lying which consists in nearly deceiving your friends without quite deceiving your enemies.'[392]

Most governments employ spin doctors to advance their causes in a good light and influence public opinion. It was Adolf Hitler who said, 'The greater the lie, the greater the chance that it will be believed.' It is a sad state of affairs to see spin doctors employed by authority figures to polish their image, but it is a situation that has woven itself into the fabric of public life.

God doesn't need a spin doctor. He is well able to represent Himself, but unfortunately some preachers do attempt to use spin doctors. The hype that proceeds some of them into a new country or city is sometimes far in excess of their calling, anointing, and ability. No doubt, we all want to be viewed in a good light and can fall into the deception of exaggeration. God's claims are real; what He says he does. Here are just a few of His claims: 'Come to Me, all you who labour and are heavy laden, and I will give you rest.'[393] 'Peace I leave with you, My peace I give to you; not as the world gives do I give to you. Let not your heart be troubled, neither let it be afraid.'[394]

Just one more will do: 'But seek first the kingdom of God and His righteousness, and all these things shall be added to you.'[395]

The problem for many Christians is that they think this is spin doctoring. How can God bless them abundantly, if they don't work all their lives from sunup to sundown? It's a good question and one that I can't answer. But it's true. Those who walk with God and honour Him will be blest. No one has to convince me that it's true. I've proved it, time and again. The Holy Spirit (God's publicist) convinced me many years ago that what God says, He means. In times of adversity, we find it difficult to believe, for we are human and subject to the weakness of self-fulfilment and often imagine that God could be the same.

This could be because we have little or no understanding of the beatific character that shall be ours in that glorious day of consummation. But it is well written and better believed that we shall have an awe-inspiring and perfectly magnificent personal state. It will not be obtained by gliding over a calm transparent transcendent sea, but by *wading through a turbulent and boisterous ocean*, windswept and jostled by contrary winds. 'For my strength is made perfect in weakness.'[396]

It will not be achieved solely by divine revelation and visions, although they may indeed be evident, but by the persisting power of the Spirit as we acquiesce to God's planned ordinance, living in submission in the destined dispensation so ordained. It is this surrender to affliction that makes us like our great high priest who was made perfect through suffering, 'For we have not an high priest which cannot be touched with the feeling of our infirmities; but was in all points tempted like as we are, yet without sin.'[397]

We are part of Christ's mystical body, the church, and cannot be above our master. We must likewise learn to tread the disruptive and cracked volcanic road. 'Although He was a Son, He learned obedience from the things which He suffered.'[398] If we would yearn for that eternal glory, we cannot exempt ourselves from maturing adversity. 'Who.' says the Bible, 'are these clothed in the white robes... 'They are the ones who come out of the great tribulation, and they have washed their robes and made them white in the blood of the Lamb.'"[399] Ours may not be *the Great Tribulation*, but all things are relative, and the current days are all tinged with distress; it is common to humanity.[400]

We may suffer unparalleled and unequal days of suffering that beggars description and subverts our faith with doubt but, although Paul had visions and revelations, God kept him located in the daily grind of normality. *The higher we reach, the deeper we could suffer.* Basically, the glory of God is manifest in the historic experience of saints as they assume the postures of patience amid their thorns!

Not the vision but the thorn

Paul looks back fourteen years to his third heaven experience; this assumes that this divine revelation was not basic to his ministry, or else he would have mentioned it earlier. His usefulness was not dependent on that heavenly exposure. Whilst some persecutors maligned his credentials, he replied about his perils and suffering; he confirmed his calling and at last mentions what others would have trumpeted earlier. But even then he adduces this special glory to a 'thorn in the flesh'.[401] He uses the thorn with the emphasis on that pain to illustrate the revelation. His physical weakness, not the heavenly visitation is prominent.

We too often become puffed up when God deals with us in mercy as we glimpse heaven. The thorn prevents us from being unduly exalted, transposing our life on earth to a transcendent and sublime experience that is divorced from everyday reality. Peter, James, and John wished to remain on transfiguration's mount, but a valley and a demon-possessed boy beckoned. The vision was a valuable insight, but a way to avoid catastrophe a thorn was provided. His thrice call was rejected. Like Cain, he lived with a mark on the flesh. Better that than to become no earthly good. *It is always difficult to synthesise the Lord's revelation without the flesh being inflated.*

My grace

God states His central truth: 'My grace is sufficient for you.'[402] Grace *was* needed, such was the soreness. And with that pain came the underfold of God. 'And my trial which was in my flesh you did not despise or reject.'[403] It was physical and evident, and because he used an amanuensis often, it is thought it was his eyes that were the problem. There is a conundrum here, for he *saw* the heavenly glories and completed his life obviously in serious discomfort.

He refers to 'the surpassing greatness of the revelations, and for this reason, to keep me from exalting myself, there was given me a thorn in the flesh, a messenger of Satan to buffet me!' Obviously, he was allowed or permitted by God to maintain humbleness. Peter's history is similar. 'Satan has desired to have you.' If all things are ours, which the Bible affirms, then so much for the thorn and the agency of administration; not only are angels working on our behalf, devils are seeking to kill and ruin us. *In the midst of that is God's eternal unwavering grace or favour.* Hallelujah!

God's grace ameliorates the pain of the thorn without removing it. God's gracious power, providence, and provision are all wrapped up in that small word – *grace*. The divine purpose is made special, for nothing is haphazard. We are the objects of concern of his omnipotence, so that it is proportionate to the thorn in its compensation. So is the glory magnified, the strength imparted. That omnipotence is manifested in grace that bears a person through appalling hardship with impossible strength and electric endeavour.

God's miracle transformation

God reached down to a sin-stricken world and recreated us as sons washed in blood and made white. He chose the most sinful and weakest and filled them with purpose, turning them from a lost eternity to a new-found system of love, joy, and peace. He was a Nazarene, rejected of men and crucified in weakness, but He rose with almighty power. *He knows about the thorn, it was His manhood.*

We fall prostrate at his feet, declaring that we have no self-righteousness, or self-sufficiency; without his forgiveness, we have no hope and are helpless. He uses the arguments we spawn against ourselves and turns them to our advantage, changing weakness into strength. 'My strength is made perfect in weakness.'[404] If you were a giant you would need to become a child. If you were wise, you'd need to become a fool. If strong, you'd become weak, and if rich, poor, for he will break all things that challenge his supremacy.

Our ground of discouragement is the very ground of hope. From it sprouts the image of God 'for when we were without strength Christ died for us.'[405] And 'where sin abounded, there does grace much more abound.'[406] But now we can cry with assurance, 'But we are strong in the Lord, and in the power of his might.'[407] Our human inadequacy is overrun by divine power, surcharged[408] by an infusion of grace.

Paul recommends a lifestyle: 'And He has said to me, "My grace is sufficient for you, for power is perfected in weakness." Most gladly, therefore, I will rather boast about my weaknesses, that the power of Christ may dwell in me.'[409] This was a complete reversal; Paul once glorified in the vision imparted on the Damascus Road, but declined to accept the thorn of sickness, asking three times for its removal. But now he rejoices in the thorn. My joy, he says by implication, is not in what I possess or have experienced of glory, for I would *rather* glory in my weakness. *Religion, from beginning to the end, is a supernatural affair.* We need to live in it.

The ultimate desire

The mark of a true believer is not the strength of a vacillating passion but a continual thirst for God. This thirst reaches upward, as it was inspired by God, and logically returns to Him. David the psalmist was a prospective Christian looking forward to a Saviour. But we are looking back, for Jesus 'ever lives to make intercession'.[410] David saw something in prophetic faith that created a thirst of magnitude, and we, looking back and also looking forward to partially see the predictive future, also have such a thirst.

The thirst that is aroused also arouses, for Moses, having seen the glory of God at the Red Sea and on the mountain with the Ten Commandments, still said, 'Show me thy glory.'[411] In similar vein, there was yet more the shepherd king desired to know. We are similar. The more we see, the more we want to see; the more we know, the more we want to know. Such was the desire created in the New Testament that the apostles, after Jesus had left on Ascension's Mount, prayed, 'Even so, come, Lord Jesus.'[412]

The fact remains, which is unavoidable, that the delights of serving and loving God increase almost exponentially. Something in the relationship born of blood inspires delight and desire and a need for deeper, richer knowledge – a yearning that is insatiable, almost a craving for consummation. Therefore, we cry with David, 'My soul thirsts for the living God.'[413]

The ultimate release

In Jeremiah, we read ten times, *'I will be thy God.'* And so He is. We do not thirst for incidental blessing from God but for God himself. It is God who forgives us, redeems us, reconciles us, and provides for us a pathway to heaven. Thus, so many who own Christ can admire him but not love him; we can be like Martha, not Mary. He provides us justice, proving our innocence; wisdom, guiding us; and mercy, enfolding us in His eternal love. That is why we seek *just* God.

Our sin has been extirpated, and yet daily we fight unnatural and unlawful passions. None of us, who are justified by Christ's blood and filled with His Holy Spirit, is exempt from sin's cloying appetites; a war subsists within. Paul says for us all so distinctly and so definitely, 'But I see another law in my members, warring against the law of my mind, and bringing me into captivity to the law of sin which is in my members.'[414] For 'I find this law at work: When I want to do good, evil is right there with me.'

Conscious of the struggle within – the pull from above and, simultaneously, the downwards drag from beneath; experiencing the antagonism of those two laws; and desirous that evil will be conquered while knowing that no human hand can touch the springs of conduct, we thirst after God. 'My heart and flesh cry out for the living God.'[415] That is where our answer lies.

The ultimate satisfaction

Living in a world that does not fully satisfy, we yearn for God because of a prevailing emptiness. All creation taken together cannot satisfy a single soul, for the more people possess, the more they are possessed by their possessions and, thus, remain unsatisfied, Such is man's capacity that, made in God's image, he needs a divine throne installed in his heart. It is there that peace reigns and joy abounds, both full of glory and spilling over.

Our joyless response amid heartbreak's bitter cup can only be sweetened and the pain assuaged by Christ's presence. Indeed, 'there is a balm in Gilead to make the wounded whole.'[416] David, who wrote this psalm, was facing bitter opposition. And yet, amid this affliction, his desire was to find Him who could sanctify the trouble. In his grievous condition, he hoped that all this would work the 'peaceable fruits of righteousness.'[417]

May we, therefore, in every avenue we walk, in every relationship we establish, in every ordinance we attempt, and in all our service be above all those things – thirsting only for Him – for all these other attractive things are substitutes. At our monthly communion, we look back to a suffering Christ. Currently, we dwell in the presence of a resurrected Saviour, and we look forward to a coming king. Those theological truths and sanctified emblems excite a thirst. But sacrament or not, truth or not, they are not sufficient. It is for God, and God alone –*it's for Him we thirst*. That is your proof, *for the man with an argument is no match for a man with an experience!*

Chapter 21

The Second Man

We have looked at our lifestyle in the midst of trial, tribulation, disappointment, disaster, disillusionment, and uncertain leading. But we should not forget that between the radiating sword in Eden and the shining eyes of the Christian are *many shades of glory*. We are being changed into that reflective glory. The faltering first steps of new birth, which have grown into the purposeful tread of a pursuing soul, have mapped a route that is tinged with the mirrored glory of a loving God. We are often unaware that He is present, yet we walk onward, seeking a destiny and not fully knowing, yet fully trusting, and finding that round the longest bend, which hides the future, shines the greatest glory.

Incidentals in life become inspirational landmarks as we suddenly find we are peeping into heaven. And there on the mount with booths and brightness, we find that Christ is revealed in the ordinary peasant garb of Galilee. Shining through, yet keeping form, the anointed one stands supreme, a transfiguration of time and flesh. He touches us repeatedly as we labour in the avenues of life, and looking up, we see in the dull greyness of a passing day, a shade of glory not seen before.

We struggle to please, and yet find we are accepted in the beloved; *labour to inherit,* when all things are ours [Italics mine]. We mistake glory for grime. And looking for something else, we miss the incarnation of Christ in the lowly and apparent worthlessness. He dwells in tabernacles not made with hands and, in His purpose, finds the dingy shelters of depraved humanity a comfortable abode. For there He brings his light – His Shekinah. The civilised litter of humankind becomes the resting place of the Spirit.

This is a story of those who suffer and yet seek glory – those who, without fully realising it, find that they are being transformed daily. They strive for that which they already possess and unwittingly find their faces begin to glow. The unconscious radiance of life bound up with God manifests purity amid iniquity, peace amid perplexity, praises amid adversity, and provision amid necessity. This fourfold claim is the rich ore of sonship, the boon of overshadowing, the blessing of infilling, and the inevitable outcome of God's overflowing.

We cannot mistake glory, for its uniqueness reveals sham and highlights the artificial, like a candle before a searchlight, a sapling before an oak, and a human before the divine. When we visit God, we always come back with more than we gave; that is the principle of the divine. Moses gave forty days yet returned fortified. He went up the mountain perspiring and came down glistening. When we meet God, we change. If we don't, we didn't. Lifestyle Christianity is the process of transforming glory, the key to change, and the door to fresh horizons.

The second man

Most of us think we want to be someone we are not. Fame flickers like a candle caught in a draught in the shadowy dimness of an advancing future, and somehow we remain as we were in the yesterday of regrets. The effort to change the inner core of what we are is a monumental task of almost unimaginable size. That iron centre of the inner self is rigid in its dominating laziness.

The prospect of mental, moral, and spiritual grandeur hops ahead of us until age strips our legs of pursuing power. We stand aside as fresh youth strides past with eager glints in their fortune-hunting eyes. It will not be long before their shoes, all dust covered, shuffle to the sidewalk and they are lost in the maze and daze of the living disillusioned. Yet, there is hope for the person who makes God his trust.

The Holy Spirit is the energising escalator by which we tread a higher route to God. But more than this, He is the life principle that restores the soul in the likeness of Christ, filling life with holy desires and practical ability to do and be what the inspired heart longs for. The residence of the Spirit from Pentecost onwards means that Saul's experience can be repeated. 'The Spirit of the Lord will come upon you, and you shall be turned into another man.'[418] What a grand stimulation that thought is—*another man*. To discard, like Peter, the failure of fireside faithlessness and turn into a rock, towering high in God's kingdom – that first-floor flood of blessing, with a hush and a rush, with the wind and a flame, was more than just an agency for power; it was the start of a new hope, with the prospect of a revolution.

What kind of man did the son of Kish become? He was already head and shoulders above his contemporaries, famous for his human frame.[419] But later, he was to be prominent for his prophetic role and kingly reign. Samuel anointed his head, and God changed his heart and, consequently, his mouth. It is with the heart that man believes unto righteousness and with his mouth that confession is made.

So, when the Holy Spirit wings His way as a beam of glory into the hub of a life, things begin to happen, but especially in the heart and from the lips. Out of the abundance of the heart, the mouth speaks. *'The heart is deceitful above all things, and desperately wicked.'*[420] We need a complete metamorphosis to become the 'second man', for the one we want to be melts past the imagination like a shadow. And though we grasp for it wildly, it slips from our fingers. God, by His Spirit, is the only one who can give that vague imagery a concrete form. And when He does, it will show through the life and lips.

The Word of God says, 'But the Spirit of the Lord came upon Gideon, and he blew a trumpet.'[421] The trumpet speaks of the gospel, but it was not until Gideon was clothed with the Spirit that a certain sound was heard. This thought is similarly expressed thus: 'And they were all filled with the Holy Ghost, and began to speak.'[422] First, comes the Spirit and then the speaking, which is the divine order. *The uncertain sound of a compromised message is the result of a breathless evangel.*

The reason Christ left the gospel in the hands of eleven weak men was that He knew that, after Pentecost, they would be different. Their friends would be astounded, and their enemies fearful. These were not the men who clung to the fringe of Calvary, like dust on the perimeter. A little maid had said to Peter, 'Surely you also are one of them, for your speech betrays you.'[423] But now, in Jerusalem itself, when he opened his mouth, who could doubt who he was? Such a floodtide came forth that the current swept 3,000 through the gates of the kingdom.[424]

These men now became the impossibles; they were impossible to quieten and impossible to refute. They paralysed the academic giants of their day with such simple yet profound logic that their accusers could only tear their clothes in anguished frustration. God had touched their hearts, and the Spirit was with each of them. Like Stephen, their lips became 'full of wisdom'.[425] The radical alteration of heart and cell structure made the listeners feel as if God was speaking to them directly – and so He was!

Science fiction has rained upon us countless theories on the possibility of aliens possessing the human race and turning the human race into cybernetic mutations. But God's transforming power is turning us back into what we once were. We are, through the Spirit, becoming like the first Adam, reigning in life and having speech that attracts divine communion. We see, in the ruins of who we are, the prospect and image of what we are becoming and realise that we shall be 'another man,' complete at the terminal transformation when Jesus comes again. 'Beloved, now we are children of God; and it has not yet been revealed what we shall be, but we know that when He is revealed, we shall be like Him, for we shall see Him as He is.'[426]

Oh yes!

Conclusion

Life in the fast lane!

Monday dawned bright, clear and sun-blue; it was one of those rare early summer days in England. It was also my day off, after the blessing of Sunday. As I often did, I awoke with ideas or thoughts about the previous day's sermon – about how it could have been developed better and the PowerPoint slides made simpler. It was hard to resist opening the programme and making corrections. And concurrently there was, as usual, a jostling for competition by thoughts about the next week's article for HICCbits – the church's weekly handout sheet.

However, bearing in mind my comments the day previously – I had preached in HICC about creative fidelity – we went to Kingston, a market town nestling on the river Thames. The old and new buildings form an appealing hard landscape, enjoyed by many as they sit in the centre drinking their beverages and enjoying the ambience created by time and industry. We strolled in the sun, enjoying the casual almost rude waste of time, absorbing the warmth and anticipating the summer in its glory, which we hoped would arrive. Possibly that Monday was the harbinger of good climate to come?

My first wife and I headed towards the river and ambled along, holding hands and chatting. As we lingered along the concrete edging peering into the brown waters, the queen's swans gathered to be fed. But we'd carried no food and they swam away, no doubt disgusted at our lack! Then we spotted a moorhen snuggled down in her nest, built in a motorbike tire and floating adjacent to a flatboat fixed to a buoy. No doubt this was a mark of her ingenuity and industry – taking the discarded flotsam of man and nature and incubating new life. Thirty metres away, we noticed a landing jetty, and underneath it, two more moorhens were building their nest. A large branch from a riverbank tree had broken off and lodged under the planks, and they were fetching and carrying twigs. One fetched, and one built, and then they reversed roles, and the other built while the first fetched. We sat on a brick wall and watched.

Then we reversed our steps, making our way towards the town centre. As we walked, we discussed new life in the church. Were we doing all that was needed and required for the people we were privileged to serve? How could we, like that moorhen, make something out of nothing that was an ingenious move of God's Spirit? What had we done over the years, and what would we do in the years to come, to see birth in the kingdom? Our undivided aim had always been to see salvation in the house and changes in individual lives. God chooses from humankind, that multinational crowd, those who were the flotsam and jetsam of humanity thrown out by human beings but who have been rescued and used by God – a floating tire here and a broken branch there, both moved by the currents of time and society. But out of that, new life has been manifest; out of nothing spectacular, so to speak, a miracle has been born.

As we sat and others stood watching this act of construction, my mind went back to the early morning. I had walked in my garden and then sat eating my breakfast in the arbour, out there in the sun enjoying the change of venue. I noticed how still everything was. I looked at the silence, and the silence looked back. And it was like that as we were on the towpath. It was as if nature was observing this building project – watching as the two birds hurriedly made their future nursery. When Halford House was built in 1908, our early church building was demolished. We salvaged five chimney pots, and they now stand in my flower border, silent terracotta sentinels destined for summer glory. We insert a small pot in the top and plant cascading flowers in them, either trailing geraniums or begonias.

They could well have been taken away and thrown carelessly into a landfill site, buried underneath tons of household rubbish. But 112 years later they still stand, not emitting smoke and soot, but displaying the wonder of English annuals. Other plants grow around them, so peeping out of that display amid the herbaceous plants and acacia trees is this bright touch of colour at about waist level – striking yet just part of the plan.

The writer of the Song of Solomon depicts the walking habits of the oriental king: 'My beloved is gone down into his garden, to the beds of spices, to feed in the gardens, and to gather lilies.'[427] And in another part, 'I went down into the garden of nuts to see the fruits of the valley, and to see whether the vine flourished, and the pomegranates budded.'[428] If he came to my garden, he would see that the rescued pots are integral in the design. The church is the garden of the Lord. And often in this garden, there are old pots, once destined for demolition but still standing, tall and strong, *bearing the marks of time*. And yet, there is also the glory of new foliage and flowers. This is God's plan indeed.

Elaborating on the term 'bearing the marks of time' would require another book in itself! The gales that accosted those old chimney pots made them valuable, as they stood against the internal and external elements and can tell their own story, some of which you have already read. *This old pot is still standing as a mark of God's mercy, faithfulness, kindness, compassion, and eternal love.* Oh yes!

The Dedication

Having referred to my first wife throughout this book, I must dedicate it to her and to her memory. To define some of Patricia's main characteristics, I must turn to the words of other writers; here are two comments from Clyde Kilby Professor of English, which describes her very well indeed.

First I'll turn to the words of Charles Williams, who said, 'I shall not allow the devilish onrush of this century to usurp all my energies but will instead fulfil the moment as the moment. I shall try to live well just now because the only time that exists is now.' She seemed not to be concerned about the future too much but about how to live and enjoy the present moment. The morning was never rushed; she dawdled over her Bible, newspapers, and breakfast. It was the current moment that captivated her. Time was in God's hand. He knew her well. She was never in haste; everything was planned and perfected in her daily programme – she had time for everything important. Other issues did not matter; they could wait.

Second, in the words of Lewis Carroll, 'I shall sometimes look back at the freshness of vision I had in childhood and try, at least for a little while, to be the child of the pure unclouded brow, and dreaming eyes of wonder.' There was a childlike simplicity about Patricia; God was sovereign of her life. What possibly could go wrong! She was His child, He her father. He loved her, and she adored Him. What could be better? She was safe; therefore, if things did apparently go wrong, there was a divine answer. God knew best. She was born into His love. He knew the future, and she trusted Him. If only we could enter into that priceless confidence and say with Edward Mote (1834):

When darkness seems to hide His face
I rest on His unchanging grace.
In every high and stormy gale
My anchor holds within the veil. *On Christ the solid rock I stand.*

If I had to make one further comment, it would be about the scriptures. Patricia was not only a woman of God; she was but a women of the Book. I expect her most valued text would be Matthew 6:23: 'Seek first the kingdom of God and all these things will be added to you.' However, she was a seer of the old school and had not only a divine presence but also a spiritual understanding beyond human intellect. A text from *The Message* would be suitable: 'Are your ears awake: Listen. Listen to the Wind Words, the Spirit blowing through the churches' (Revelation 3:2). She heard – heard from God constantly. In spite of all her suffering, she always pointed me to my duty to God. Nothing was allowed to interfere with God's will. Hers is a legacy unparalleled.

Bibliography (mostly scripture) Usually New King James Version

1   Job 5:7

2   Mark 9:24

3   Deut. 21:17

4   Judson Cornwall, Profiles of leadership, Bridge-Logos Publishers, 1 Jan 1980

5   Laura Spinney, 'The Killer Bean of Calabar', *New Scientist*, 28 June 2003, 48.

6   Ps. 108:12

7   Acts 9:1, 2

8   Acts 9:21

9   Ps. 341, NEB

10   Jas. 1: 22

11   Luke 15

12   Matt. 18:20

13   Romans 8:35

14   Tim Butcher, *Daily Telegraph*, Monday, 18 January 1998, 7.

15   2 Cor. 1:22

16   John 10 28

17   Isa. 49:16

18   Isa. 53:11

19   Matt. 5:4

20   A paraphrase of notes by William Barclay Daily Study Notes. Pub. The Westminster Press Philidelphia. 1958

21   Phil. 4:7

22   The Message-NKJV Parallel Bible copyright 1982. Thomas Nelson, Inc. PAGE 1384 - Matthew 5:4

23   John 11:21

24   John 11:5

25   John 11:39

26   1 Cor. 13:11

27   Isa. 42:3

28   Matt. 17:1 ff

29   Deut. 19:15

30   Luke 9:31

31   1 Cor. 15:52

32   1 Tim. 4:16

33   Acts 1:11

34   John 20:16

35   Luke 24:31

36   John 20:27

37   Revelation 1

38   2 Cor. 3:18

39   Ps. 93:2

40   1 John 3:2

41   Albert Einstein

42   Eccles. 3:2

43   Matthew 10:38

44   Shakia Ahmed, Tarvelalodge. July 2010 6,000 adults surveyed

45   2 Cor. 1:3

46   Luther Bridgers, first pub March 26th 1911.

47   Eccles. 7:10

48   Heb. 6:12

49   Isiah 46:4

50   We are told that God is within us 163 times in the New Testament.

51   Daily Telegraph

52   Eccles. 11:5

53   Ps. 139:13

54   Luke 23:46

55   Rev. 1:14, TLB

56   Dan. 10:6, NIV

57   Job 31:4

58   2 Sam. 12:7

59   John 1:48

60   Luke 19:5

61   John 4:16

62   The Telegraph Newspaper. 23rd September 2011. No author indicated.

63   Mark 14:8

64   Eccles. 7:14

65   Daily Telegraph 2006

66   Bob Wilson, Behind the Network. Pub. Hodder Paperbooks 2004

67   Rom. 5:3–4, *The Message*

68   2 Cor. 4:17

69   Eccles. 7:14

70   Lam. 3:1

71   Lam. 1:12

72   1 Cor. 10:13

73   1 Pet. 1:2

74   1 Pet. 4:12–13
75   John 16:33
76   Ps. 34:19
77   Rom. 12:1
78   Ps. 119:59
79   Rom. 18:31
80   Heb. 12:3
81   George Matheson, 'O Love That Wilt Not Let Me Go', 1882.
82   Eccles. 7:14
83   1 Pet. 5:6–7
84   1 Sam. 3:18
85   Rev. 2:4
86   Hos. 6:4
87   Job. 8:20
88   2 Cor. 3:18
89   Prov. 14:14
90   Job 34: 31–32
91   L. F. W. Woodford, 'Burn Fire of God'.
92   Heb. 2:10
93   2 Cor. 5:21
94   Matthew 20:23
95   Galatians 3:26
96   H. G. Wells, Experiement in Autobiography. Discoveries and
     Conclusions of a Very Ordianry Brain. Pub. Chuck Greif & the
     OnlineProofreading Team. 1934
97   Gen. 37:19
98   Heb. 10:36, TLB
99   Isa. 24:15, KVJ
100   Heb. 12:2
101   Job 19:20
102   Job 7:4
103   Isa. 24:15, KVJ
104   Ps. 66:12
105   Isa. 43:2
106   1 Pet. 4:12
107   Job 5:6–7
108   Ps. 34:19
109   Heb. 5:8–9
110   Col. 1:18
111   Isa. 53:3
112   Heb. 12:6

113 Rev. 3:1–2
114 Job 35:10
115 Mic. 7:7
116 Ps. 61:2
117 Ps. 79:13
118 Luke 19:40
119 1 Pet. 2:9
120 Job 1:21
121 Ps. 145:17
122 Ps. 119:75
123 Heb. 12:9–10
124 Gen. 18:14
125 Heb. 13:8
126 Rom. 4:20
127 Ps. 78:41
128 Ps. 77:10
129 Acts 17:28
130 Ps. 139:2
131 Mark 14:8
132 2 Cor. 12:9–10
133 Isa. 53:4–5
134 John 12:24
135 Australian Financial Review, 16thMay 2000
136 Acts 12:16
137 Phil. 4:13
138 Ps. 138:3
139 Joel 3:10
140 Preachers over many years.
141 Gen. 32:25
142 Malcom Gladwell, The Tipping Point. Pub Little, Brown and Company.
    March 2000
143 Phil. 4:11–13, TLB
144 2 Cor. 12:8
145 Acts 3:6
146 Matt. 14:25
147 Matt. 14:34
148 1 Pet. 2:9–11
149 Heb 4:16
150 Isaiah 43:16
151 'It Is Well with My Soul' is a well-known hymn by Horatio G. Spafford.
152 Luke 21:19

153 Ps. 76:10

154 John 21:11

155 Isa. 59:19

156 Isiah 43:16

157 Heb. 2:10

158 Ps. 77:19

159 2 Cor. 5:7

160 2 Cor. 4:17–18

161 Prov. 14:30

162 Acts 7:9

163 Jas. 3:16

164 Griffith Thomas, *Genesis: A Devotional Commentary* (Grand Rapids: Wm B. Eerdmans Pub. Co.,1946), 362.

165 Gen. 39:19–23

166 Phil. 1:12–13, from Matthew Henry's Commentary

167 Psalm 105:17-24

168 Charles H. Spurgeon, *The Treasury of the Old Testament* vol. 1 (Grand Rapids: Baker Book House Company, 1988), 182.

169 Acts 7:9

170 Gen. 5:22

171 Num. 12:3

172 John 20:2

173 Luke 7:28

174 Acts 3:22

175 Gen. 48:5

176 Gen. 39:3, 23; 41: 38

177 Eccles. 12:1

178 Ps. 12:6

179 From The Holy Bible: New International Version. Copyright © 1973, 1978, 1984, by International Bible Society - 2 Peter 3:5–7.

180 Dan. 4:35

181 Job 23:13

182 Eph. 1:11

183 Jer. 29:11

184 Job 3:25

185 2 Chr. 11:14

186 2 Chr. 15:3

187 Neh. 5:17

188 Acts 27:8

189 Matt. 16:21–22

190 Ps. 37:1

191   Isa. 53:12
192   1 Pet. 5:7
193   Phil 4:6
194   Gen. 1:1–2
195   Eph. 2:1
196   Gen. 11:31; 12:9
197   Matt. 14:28–31
198   Genesis 37
199   Genesis 39–41
200   Genesis 27
201   Gen. 28: 10–17
202   Rev. 3:8
203   Acts 14:27
204   1 Cor. 16:9
205   1 Cor. 3:10
206   Rev. 3:20
207   John 6:16 ff
208   By Harriet Barovick, Tam Gray, Daniel S. Levy, Lina Lofaro, David
      Spitz, Flora Tartakovsky and Chris Taylor, Tourism, *Time Magazine*, 22
      February 1999.
209   Acts 17:28
210   Luke 12:33–34
211   Gen. 3:15
212   Acts 2:23
213   Prov. 13:12
214   Ps. 37:7
215   Ps. 37:9
216   Gen. 12:1
217   Gen. 12:3
218   Gen. 12:3
219   Ps. 22:1
220   John 17:11
221   Matt. 20:28
222   John 3:16
223   Ps. 105:17–18
224   Gen. 37:5
225   Ps. 76:10
226   John 11:14
227   John 11:25
228   Ps. 27:14
229   Ps. 62:5

230   Ps. 37:34
231   Isa. 30:18
232   Ephesians 4:22-24
233   Heb. 2:1
234   Hos. 11:8. James Moffatt translation of the Bible, New York:Doran, 1926. Revised Edfition, New York and London: harper and Brothers, 1935 reprinted, Grnad rapids: Kregsl, 1995
235   Matheson, 'O Love'.
236   Jennie Evelyn Hussey, 'Lead Me to Calvary', 1921.
237   A. W. Tozer, *The Knowledge of the Holy* (Harper Collins Publishers, 1961), preface.
238   Eccles. 1:14
239   Eph. 5:27
240   Andrew Murray, The Certainty of Answer to Prayer, *Discipleship Magazine* 1995 page 53.
241   1 Cor. 13:7 ff
242   Gen. 4:6
243   1 Kgs. 19:9
244   Matt. 26:50
245   John 21:15
246   Acts 9:4
247   Matt. 25:23
248   Psa. 103:1
249   Eph. 4:3
250   1 Tim. 5:22
251   Jas. 1:27
252   1 John 5:21
253   Prov. 24:26
254   John 15: 3–15
255   Prov. 18:24
256   Gal. 4:6–7
257   Proverbs 23:18
258   Ps. 62:5
259   Ephesians 2:3
260   Eph. 2:3
261   S. of S. 2:4
262   Ps. 37:37
263   Rom. 6:22
264   Matt. 19:29
265   Rom. 8:17
266   Isa. 53:11

267   1 Pet. 2:2

268   Mark 8:24

269   2 Cor. 1:22

270   Rev. 21:27

271   Rom. 6:14

272   Rom. 16:20

273   Isa. 54:17

274   1 Cor. 13:12

275   Rom. 8:28

276   Isiah 65:24

277   Jon Henley, Keep Calm and carry On, The Guardian newspaper, 18th March 2009

278   Isa. 9:16

279   Prov. 18:24

280   Frank Damazio, *Successful Leadership* (Portland: Bible Temple Publications, 1993), 138.

281   Rev. 3:18

282   Luke 19:20

283   Prov. 22:29

284   Rev. 3:18

285   Rev. 5:9

286   1 Cor. 4:9

287   1 Pet. 1:7

288   Job 23:10

289   Prov. 17:3

290   1 Kgs. 22:3

291   John Lawleee & Jonathan Petre, 'Chusssh, Chusssh, Chusssh' sounds righ note for safety, 22nd Juky 2001, Then Telegraph.

292   Acts 2:2

293   Acts 2:6

294   Job 26:14

295   1 Cor. 13:12

296   S. of S. 1:4

297   1 Pet. 5:8

298   2 Cor. 11:14

299   1 Cor. 13:10

300   John Avanzini, *Always Abounding* (Harrison House), 1983.

301   Prov. 11:24–25

302   Matthew 26:12

303   Matt. 8:15

304   2 Cor. 4:18

305 Henry Wadsworth Longfellow

306 Prov. 13:12

307 John 10:10

308 Martin Luther King used the words, 'I have a dream' in a number of speeches, most famously in the one he delivered in Washington on 27 August 1963.

309 Isa. 53:11

310 Phil. 3:14

311 Heb. 6:12

312 Matt. 24:12; Rev. 12:9, 12

313 1 Cor. 15:58

314 Heb. 10:38

315 2 Sam. 1:17–18

316 2 Sam. 12:23

317 John 21:3

318 Acts 17:28

319 Isa. 40:31

320 Luke 21:19

321 Heb. 10:36, TLB

322 Gen. 28:12

323 Gen. 28:16

324 George Bush, 'Quotes of the Week', *The Sunday Times*, 16 October 1988

325 Gen. 37:19–20

326 Rom. 11:29

327 Phil. 1:6

328 Phil. 2:13

329 2 Cor. 2:14; Rom. 8: 37

330 1 Cor. 3:7

331 2 Cor. 3:1

332 1 John 4:4

333 Obituaries, 'Elizabeth Mortimer', *Daily Telegraph*, 26 August 1997, 19.

334 Ps. 71:18

335 Dan. 3:18, TLB

336 William Shakespeare (1564–1616), *Hamlet* vol. 2.

337 *The Treasury of Scripture Knowledge* (Marshall Morgan & Scott), page 363.

338 Matt. 6:33

339 1 Tim. 6:6

340 Ps. 84:11

341 Oswald Sanders, *On to Maturity* (Marshall, Morgan & Scott), 63.

342 Heb. 11:36–40, TLB

343 Ps. 73:2

344 Isa. 43:2, TLB

345 Zech. 13:9, TLB

346 Acts 14:22

347 Olga Craig, *Sunday Telegraph*, 17.

348 Heb. 4: 15

349 Matt. 25:40

350 Jas. 4:3

351 Alexander Pope in James Stewart, *Walking with God*, 101.

352 Heb. 13:12

353 Matt. 8:15

354 Robert Browning (1812–89), British poet, *Andrea del Sarto*

355 Jennie Churchill in a letter to her son Winston Churchill, 26 February 1897, in Ralph G. Martin's *Jennie: The Life of Lady Randolph Churchill* vol. 2.

356 Niccolo Machiavelli

357 Phil. 3:10–14

358 Oswald Chambers, Our Portrait in Genesis, 1957 by Oswald Chambers Publishing Association Limted.

359 Hosea 12:12

360 Rom. 6:23

361 John 3:16

362 Ps. 4:8

363 Ps. 91:6

364 John Henry Jowett, *Things that Matter Most: Devotional Papers* (New York: Fleming H. Revell Company, 1913), 189.

365 2 Sam. 12:7

366 Eph. 4:32

367 Gen. 50:17

368 Ruth 2:3

369 Ruth 2:20

370 Luke 1:78

371 Fred Pearce, 'Histories: Pyramids of Dew', *New Scientist*, 13 April 2005.

372 Gen. 27:28

373 Isa. 26:19

374 Jowett, *Things that Matter*, 192.

375 Psalm 91:1–6

376 Dan. 3:25

377 Jessica Berens, The agony and the ecstasy, The Observer May 2002

378 Rom. 15:4

379 Isa. 5:5

380   Job 1:10
381   Hos. 2:6
382   Jer. 2:19
383   Heb. 13:5
384   1 John 2:15
385   Hos. 4:17
386   Ps. 8:4
387   1 Sam. 12:21
388   S. of S. 1:4
389   Sweet & Frank Viola, The Jesus Manifesto, pub. Thomas Nelson - 2010
390.   Ephesians 2:13
391.   Luke 10:42
392.   Francis MacDonald Cornford
393.   Matt. 11:28
394.   John 14:27
395.   Matt. 6:33
396.   2 Cor. 12:9 NKJV
397.   Heb. 4:15
398.   Heb. 5:8
399.   Rev. 7:13–14
400.   Job 5:7
401.   2 Cor. 12:7
402.   2 Corinthians 12:9
403.   Gal. 4:14
404.   2 Cor. 12:9
405.   Rom. 5:6
406.   Rom. 5:20
407.   Eph. 6:10
408.   To over stamp existing currency [postage stamp] so as to increase its face value though postage and delvery.
409.   2 Cor. 12:9–10
410.   Rom. 8:34
411.   Exod. 33:18
412.   Rev. 22:20
413.   Ps. 42:2
414.   Rom. 7:23
415.   Ps. 84:2
416.   Black-American spiritual. The "balm in Gilead" is a reference from the Old Testament -- Jeremiah 8:22
417.   Heb. 12:11
418.   1 Sam. 10:6

419. 1 Sam. 9:2
420. Jer. 17:9
421. Judg. 6:34
422. Acts 2:4
423. Matt. 26:73
424. Acts 2:41
425. Acts 6:3
426. 1 John 3:2, NKJ
427. S. of S. 6:2
428. S. of S. 6:11
429. 1 John 4:4
430. Ecclesiastes 7:14

CPSIA information can be obtained
at www.ICGtesting.com
Printed in the USA
LVOW08s1028190317
527715LV00001B/288/P